# MEASURE YOUR SUCCESS
# IN MOMENTS

## SAM BURGETT

Joshua Tree
Publishing

• Chicago •

# MEASURE YOUR SUCCESS IN MOMENTS
## SAM BURGETT

*Published by*
### Joshua Tree Publishing
### • Chicago •
JoshuaTreePublishing.com

13-Digit ISBN: 978-1-956823-40-0

Front Cover Image Credit: Alpar-Adobe Stock

# Disclaimer:

This book is designed to provide information about the subject matter covered. The opinions and information expressed in this book are those of the author, not the publisher. Every effort has been made to make this book as complete and as accurate as possible. However, there may be mistakes both typographical and in content. Therefore, this text should be used only as a general guide and not as the ultimate source of information. The author and publisher of this book shall have neither liability nor responsibility to any person or entity with respect to any loss or damage caused or alleged to be caused directly or indirectly by the information contained in this book.

Printed in the United States of America

# DEDICATION

Thank you to all who are taking the time to read this book and are seeking to understand the experiences of those who are often thrown away by society.

Thank you to everyone who has supported the Community Change Center, which allows me to continue doing this work.

Most importantly, thank you to the youth and young adults who allowed me to not only work with and learn from them but to share their stories, in hopes of shedding light on this important issue and humanizing a population which is so deeply stigmatized in America.

Thank you to John Paul Owles and Joshua Tree Publishing for taking a chance on me, to the editing team, and to everyone who has supported me throughout this journey.

"Hurt people,
hurt people."

~

Anonymous

# TABLE OF CONTENTS

# PREFACE

Throughout the years I have spent working within the juvenile and adult justice systems, a large component of my work has involved simply trying to humanize my clients to a society that has largely demonized currently and formerly-incarcerated people. There are approximately 1.8 million adults incarcerated in the United States, including people in jails and prisons (Vera, 2021). Additionally, over 48,000 young people throughout the United States are held in secure facilities, including detention centers, group homes, residential treatment facilities, prisons and jails, and long-term secure facilities, due to involvement in the juvenile and/or adult justice systems. Approximately 16,858 young people are incarcerated within juvenile detention centers daily throughout the country, containing disproportionate numbers of youth of color (Sawyer, 2019).

A majority of the currently and formerly incarcerated population have either diagnosed or undiagnosed mental illness and/or have experienced abuse, neglect, and other forms of significant trauma. Backgrounds of justice-involved juveniles frequently indicate abuse and victimization, an unsteady home life, death or loss, and early trauma.

Numerous studies have demonstrated that trauma impairs a person's ability to self-regulate, often causing them to view the world as hostile and to not trust others. Trauma also causes self-destructive behavior and hinders coping skills. With this knowledge, it is clear that a person's history and experiences greatly impact their behavior. Often those who victimize others have been victimized themselves and had numerous negative experiences throughout their childhood and early adolescence (Baer, 2003). As my colleagues and I often remind ourselves and others, "Hurt people hurt people."

While we often allow a mistake and resulting felony conviction to create barriers that a person must overcome for the rest of their life, we fail to recognize that person as someone's brother, sister, spouse, neighbor, friend, or child. We often bar individuals with certain felonies from public housing, rental units, the labor market, certain licensures and certifications (the list goes on), not considering that these people are our fellow community members. Many of them have survived and overcome experiences that many of us who have not encountered the justice system could not imagine.

The primary goal of this book is to highlight the humanity among people who have been discarded by society and who are often viewed—and even view themselves—as unworthy or bad. Moreover, I aim to promote understanding and knowledge of the barriers faced by a majority of the population—barriers that have led to their arrests and rearrests and cycling in and out of the justice system. Lastly, I hope this book inspires change. With the recognition that most of those involved in the justice system never had a fair chance at a good, healthy, happy life, I hope all readers use this opportunity to gain empathy and understanding toward those we often write off and throw away as a society. By the end of this book, I hope you will be equipped to help shift the narrative surrounding our incarcerated and formerly-incarcerated neighbors.

Note: All names included in this study have been changed to ensure confidentiality is upheld.

# INTRODUCTION

Having moved to a new town in 2016 for college and accepted a job working as a cashier at Menards the week prior, I felt unfulfilled and bored. Because I grew up in a small, rural town where I had founded and run a mentoring program and was used to being known by everyone and feeling needed by the kids in my program, I was discomforted by this new feeling of being unknown and largely unneeded. I googled local nonprofits where I could volunteer my free time and found myself sitting in the parking lot of the Boys and Girls Club just a few miles away from my new university. I walked into the old, looming building, unsure of what I would say when I entered but certain that I was in the right place.

Upon walking through the front doors, I immediately recognized the receptionist from one of my social work classes at the university. Feeling more comfortable at the sight of a familiar face, I approached the desk and explained to my classmate that I was looking to do some volunteer work with youth.

"We need a teen room person," she informed me. "Do you want to get paid or work for free?"

Within the next three weeks, I interviewed, trained, and found myself alone in a room full of teenagers who seemed wary yet excited to finally have a staff member assigned to their room.

A small fire, several outings, many long talks, and a lot of relationship-building later, I found myself referring to the teens as "my kids," and they seemed to accept me as the new teen room staff. Constantly confided in when my girls wanted to "spill the tea" and share the current drama at their schools, always attempting to resolve arguments between one pair of twin girls, aiming to provide helpful advice to the recounts of daily struggles unloaded by many of the youth when they plopped down in my room when they arrived at the club after school, I was invigorated by my sense of obligation to watch out for the teens.

I made a purposeful attempt to always keep an extra close eye on one of my boys, Charlie, who was known throughout the club to have a rough home life. Charlie's mother was not present in his life, and it was impossible not to notice his dirty clothes, hair that desperately needed trimming, and unclean odor when he arrived at the club every day, often after riding his bike for miles from his school or home. Emotionally delayed, Charlie did not always pick up on social cues and had a desperate need for attention from staff, other youth, and the weekly girlfriends that he would make a show of announcing when they called or texted him.

As a result of his lack of social graces, many of the other teens made a point to ignore or make fun of him. When Charlie arrived on his Razor scooter one day, he proudly rode it into my room and informed me that he was riding the scooter because the chain on his bike was broken. One of the wealthy teen boys looked at the scooter in disgust, stating, "Eww, what is THAT? It looks like it belongs to a poor person."

I saw shame flash across Charlie's face, briefly, before he could shrug and simply exit the room as if the other boy's comment did not hurt him. Ignored and made fun of by many other club members, Charlie began acting out more and more to gain attention. As other members began to distance themselves from him more, Charlie's behaviors became increasingly obnoxious.

When Charlie did not appear in my room one day, I asked around the club at the end of the day to see if any other staff members had seen him. "No, I haven't seen him," was the common response. I assured myself that kids missed days at the club all the time and that it was no big deal. However, I could not help but wonder and worry as I left work for the day. After nearly three weeks had passed with no sighting of Charlie, he came sauntering downstairs to the teen room.

"Where have you been?" I questioned.

"I got locked up," he said loudly enough for the other teens to hear. As he gained the attention of several other teens in the room, he explained how he was arrested, transported to juvie in handcuffs, and locked up with other "bad kids."

As Charlie spoke, he purposefully threw in curse words at a minimum of every other sentence. When I reminded him that we did not use that language in the room, he remarked, "Do you know where I've been? I can't help it!"

Charlie's behaviors spiraled over the next several months, and he was arrested for probation violations on numerous accounts. Staff grew increasingly frustrated with his worsening behaviors, and other club members went out of their way to make it apparent that they did not like Charlie. Simultaneously, Charlie put in constant effort to continue growing his reputation as "tough." Nearly a daily occurrence, Charlie would walk into my room with his drawstring bag and comment on the cigarettes in his pocket, the marijuana he had smoked the night prior, or the trouble he was in at his school. As he made such remarks, he would glance at me to evaluate my reaction. He craved my apparent disapproval, partially because he enjoyed the attention and partially because my chastisement was a sign that I cared. Charlie began to appear less frequently at the Boys and Girls Club, although each day that he did, he would come to the teen room to give me a hug and hear my "be smart and safe" lecture.

As months passed, a similar pattern began to emerge among two of my other teens. They seemed to be alternating periods of short-term incarceration, constantly returning to the club with stories of their days spent in juvie. One day, all three of my then juvenile-justice-system-involved kids came into the teen room together. Charlie had decided that he was now gang-affiliated, and he threw up a hand signal. One of the other teens watched the gesture and remarked under his breath but loudly enough for Charlie to hear, "Oh my god, was that supposed to be the Blood sign? He didn't even do it right," as he snickered in Charlie's direction.

Aware of the extremely low probability that Charlie had any type of association with the Bloods (a well-known gang but with little to no presence in the area), I was conscious of Charlie's immature attempts to gain attention and friends by donning the mask of having power through involvement in illegal activities. Over the next few months, I watched my three kids cycle in and out of detention, putting the mask of being "hard" on around other teens and occasionally taking it off when I pulled them aside to ask how they were doing.

One day, one of my girls appeared at the club and informed us that when she was in the detention center the day prior, Charlie had been there as well. Tired of seeing the kids continue down the path of frequent lockups and increasingly negative behaviors after being released from detention, I asked my boss, the club's program director, Luke, if he would be willing to go visit Charlie in the detention center with me. I looked up the facility's visitation policy online and informed my boss that visitors had to call and schedule a visit. We determined that we would attempt to visit anyway, as it was already too late to schedule a visit for the day.

We left work at 8:30 p.m. and headed to the detention center, less than ten miles away from the club. We entered the glass door, and I was thankful that Luke was there to do the talking, as I was immediately intimidated by the voice that came over the loudspeaker when Luke pushed the intercom button on the wall. After Luke explained who we were and that we were hoping to visit Charlie, the voice stated, "The kids are already in bed, and only family can visit anyway." Disappointed, we thanked the voice and left the facility. However, I left with a sense that I had to learn more about why our kids were constantly cycling in and out of the detention facility.

The week after attempting to visit Charlie in the detention center, I asked one of my classmates from my criminological theory class, Abby, if she would be interested in starting up some type of mentoring group at the local juvenile detention center with me. She said she would be interested in helping initiate the project, so I mentioned our idea to one of our criminology professors, who had initially inspired me to begin studying the justice system. Our professor loved the idea and set up a meeting with the detention center director for the four of us to meet and discuss potentially starting the program. Before we knew it, we had a start-up date for our Saturday mentoring program in the juvenile detention center.

Using the money we had from our part-time jobs, mine at the Boys and Girls Club and Abby's at a limo-detailing company, we purchased chips and pop and planned a career-interest activity to complete with the detention center residents in our first Saturday session. Although I was confident and comfortable in working with the teen population, I admittedly was nervous to co-facilitate our first session at the facility, unsure of how the residents would respond to a few college students coming in and attempting to run a mentoring session with them.

On the first Saturday that we were scheduled to begin the program, Abby, a third facilitator with whom we were friends, and I walked into the detention center, loaded with papers, chips, and two liters of pop, and we nervously pressed the intercom button.

"Can I help you?" asked the voice over the intercom.

"Hi, we're students here for the mentoring program," I responded into the speaker.

We heard a door click to the left and followed the voice's instructions to go into the waiting room. Placing our belongings into the lockers and trying not to make it apparent that we had never entered a detention center before, we signed in and provided our IDs to the detention officer that came to retrieve us. After passing through a metal detector and three additional doors, we found ourselves in what we later learned to call the Multipurpose Room, or the MPR, with approximately fifteen residents, primarily male, sitting around tables and staring at us curiously.

We introduced ourselves and explained that we were excited to begin running a Saturday program at the facility. I asked the residents to introduce themselves to us as well. As the youth went around the room stating their names, I noted the khaki-colored pants, white sweatshirts, and black sandals that each resident was wearing. In my head, I kept thinking, "These kids are incarcerated. These are the kids that society is afraid of. These are the kids that our community does not like." However, as the teens went around introducing themselves, I was aware that aside from the setting, there was nothing different about these teenagers in comparison to my teens at the Boys and Girls Club.

While we did provide snacks, I was conscious of the fact that we were asking the kids involved in our mentoring group to do work on a Saturday rather than watching the movies that they were enjoying before we arrived to facilitate the session. However, rather than complaining, the kids were excited, invested, and clearly craved the attention. An hour and a half later, we concluded the session and told the residents that we had to leave.

"When are you coming back?" many of the group participants questioned. "Thank you for coming!" "That was really fun," we heard as one of the officers led us back out of the room, and the kids waved goodbye.

After nearly six months of our biweekly Saturday mentoring groups, I was ready to become more involved. I looked so forward to our mentoring sessions and enjoyed the residents immensely. I submitted an application to the detention center for a position as a detention officer. Because I had already established rapport with the director of the facility, I emailed her one week after submitting the application to check on its status. She called me the next day, stating, "I had not seen that you submitted an app. When can you come interview?"

The week before Christmas break of my junior year of college, I completed an interview at the facility and began my eighty hours of training the following week.

Once I had completed the paperwork components of my orientation, I was allowed on the floor with the residents. As soon as I walked out on a weekday wearing the uniform "Juvenile Detention Center" sweatshirt, the kids' eyes grew wide, and they exclaimed in disbelief, "You work here now? Does this mean you can give us points during group?" The point system was utilized as a behavior management system, with residents losing points and, therefore, privileges as a result of negative behaviors, such as disrespect and failing to follow instructions.

The longer I worked with the residents at the detention center, the more I came to recognize the gaps and structural issues within the juvenile justice system. However, I also learned a great deal about the enormous stigma that is attached to those who are or who have been incarcerated, regardless of age. As I talked with people about my work within the facility, some of the most common questions were: "Aren't you scared?" and "Are there a lot of fights?" Telling humanizing stories about the youth detained within the facility in an attempt to combat the stigma that people who had never met them attached to the youth, simply as a result of their justice involvement, became a daily routine for me. The harder I tried to combat the stigma that society placed upon the youth I was working with in the facility, the more I became invested in working with and advocating for the justice-involved population.

After co-facilitating the mentoring program within the detention center for nearly a year and having worked as a detention officer for several months, I became increasingly disturbed by the recidivism among the youth. Many of them would be detained for several weeks to several months, be released from the facility, and return weeks, days, or even hours later. In an attempt to address this systemic issue, I set out to create an evidence-based reentry program that could be implemented within juvenile detention facilities. After months of researching other successful youth reentry programs, traveling to Norway, where I studied their justice system, and discussing logistics with the detention center administration, I designed Project REACH. I began implementing the program three times per week within the facility in September 2019, incorporating group sessions as well as individual meetings with participating youth. Three times weekly, I met separately with the older and younger groups of youth as we completed the curriculum that I had designed. First, we focused on self-esteem, then decision-making, then setting goals, and finally, how we could go about achieving their goals. The REACH curriculum was designed to comprehensively empower the youth and prepare them for success upon their release from incarceration.

In addition to meeting in our groups, I met individually with youth when they were ready to begin setting individual goals or when they just wanted someone to listen to them more privately than within the group setting. Through our group sessions and particularly through our one-on-one sessions, I watched youth let the walls they had built up around themselves come tumbling down as they realized it was alright to be vulnerable. The other immense benefit to Project REACH is that the program allowed me to provide youth with the opportunity to continue receiving services upon their release from detention.

Under the umbrella of Project REACH, I had the unique privilege of being able to provide the youth with the option to connect with me post-incarceration so we could continue working together to achieve their goals. Through the implementation of the program, both within the juvenile detention center and out within the community, I had the privilege of building relationships with the youth and young adults described throughout this book. While the statistical analysis of Project REACH shows that the program was able to effectively provide youth with increased feelings of a sense of support, improved self-esteem, and a better understanding of their goals and how they should go about working to achieve their goals, I will always recognize that the youth who fully engaged in this program taught me far more than I ever could have hoped to teach them.

In 2019, I founded a nonprofit organization, The Community Change Center: WeAreOne, Inc., which has allowed me to obtain funding and additional resources to provide such reentry resources on a larger scale. Located in Northwest Indiana, we work with individuals during their incarceration and continue providing wraparound services as they reintegrate back into the community. Such services include transitional living reentry housing, adult education, a Unity Café which promotes social interaction among diverse groups, mentoring and case management services, and recurring expungement fairs for individuals who qualify for expungement of their record but cannot afford to hire an attorney. Through the Community Change Center, I have been able to engage with greater numbers of individuals, both youth and adults, during and post-incarceration throughout the community.

# CHAPTER 1

# HECTOR

Around one year into my work at the detention center as a detention officer, a seventeen-year-old named Hector returned for his fourth period of incarceration at our facility. Even with his full, curly hair, which puffed out at least two inches on all sides, Hector was hardly 5' 3" tall. When I first met Hector, I was impressed by his politeness and his sense of wanting a better life for himself. As I commonly did with the residents, I introduced myself and asked him when his court hearing was. He informed me of the date and stated that he was really hoping to be ordered to serve a commitment, a period of anywhere from 30 to 120 days in the juvenile detention center but was expecting to be sent back to the Department of Correction (DOC), otherwise known as Boys' School, where he had previously served two years.

Because DOC houses individuals with the most maladaptive, dangerous behaviors that have not been corrected in less restrictive settings, Hector matter-of-factly stated that he knew he would go back to his "old ways" of fighting and not caring what happened to him if he was sent back to DOC. Impressed by his self-awareness, determined attitude, and kind heart, I made constant attempts to convey these characteristics to the court in my contact notes in his file. Hector received the commitment that he had asked for and was spared serving another sentence at DOC. For a couple of weeks, Hector studied for his TASC (Test Assessing Secondary Completion), or high school equivalency exam, and he continued to be a model resident in the facility. About one month into his commitment, an apparent shift occurred as Hector began to grow bored of the same daily routine and became tired of other residents viewing him as "soft."

One evening, as we were eating dinner in the secure dining room, one resident was mocking another boy for liking the somewhat famous rapper Lil Skies' music. Hector, standing up for the resident currently under scrutiny by the other boys, remarked, "Hey! Lay off my boy, Jordan!" Jordan snapped back at Hector, "I can take care of myself, bro!" Hector, attempting to hide his hurt, remarked back, "See if I ever stand up for you again, bro!" Amused yet concerned for Jordan and Hector's hidden feelings, I watched the interaction and the manifestation of the common belief among the incarcerated teenage boys that "kindness is weakness."

Over the following weeks, Hector began talking more and more about his gang (known to be the Latin Kings), guns, and drugs. He also began getting into trouble with staff more frequently for disrespect and not following instructions. Throughout the following month, I noticed Hector's behavior becoming worse and worse, leading to several suspensions, or twenty-four-hour periods in his cell, for non-threatening behaviors seeming to stem from his deep desire to gain respect and prove himself and a craving for attention. However, as Hector's behavior grew worse, the staff grew less hopeful that he would obtain his TASC while detained or that he would be successful upon release. The staff's decreasing interest in helping Hector seemed to also decrease his own motivation to do well.

Every day when I arrived at work and went to complete a guard tour, a mandatory check of every cell to make sure no residents were trying to harm or kill themselves, Hector would crouch down under his door and jump up in an attempt to scare me when I looked into his cell. Regardless of whether or not he successfully startled me, he would break into a huge, delighted, child-like grin each time he popped up and saw me at his door. Commonly described as a "career criminal" by several staff members at the facility, I saw the boy inside that just wanted unconditional love and attention. As is common among members of gangs or groups, I suspected that Hector likely became affiliated in order to find a sense of belonging and support that was missing from his life otherwise.

Although he had begun sagging his pants lower and lower, using more "street talk," and acting more disrespectful and "hard" over the course of his stay at the facility, I frequently noticed the quick glances Hector would make when other older youth, whom he wanted to impress, came into the facility. For example, while we were watching the movie *Aladdin* one night, each time Hector laughed at a scene, he would quickly glance over to see if the new resident who, like Hector, had spent years in the DOC, found the scene funny too. Each time Hector was speaking about or doing something he knew was against the facility rules, he would quickly glance at the staff members in the room. When he would see me raising an eyebrow in his direction with my arms crossed toward him, he would grin, raise his own eyebrows, throw his arms up in the air, and innocently shout, "What, Sam?"

A couple of months into his stay at the facility, Hector had two felony charges filed against him for making threats against staff. With the realization that he was likely either going to be sent to DOC for years or waived to adult court and sent to the county jail, Hector's behavior only grew worse. Still clinging to the hope that I could get through to him and help him see hope for himself and his life, I began meeting with him individually to continue setting goals and encouraging him to work toward these goals. For days in a row, I went to the detention center on the days when I was not scheduled to work, pulled him out of class, and simply talked with him. Hector was adamant that no one was in his corner and that he had wasted his entire life being stupid and being repeatedly locked up. "Ain't nobody care about us in here," was Hector's common statement during many of our meetings. I frequently reminded Hector that he was only seventeen years old and could have an entire life ahead of him. As Hector had previously and repeatedly told me that he did not believe he would live past age twenty, he was hesitant to entertain the possibility that he could have some type of life once he was released.

We continued our daily chats, and as we sat and he talked about his past, present, and potential future, I could see the sorrow apparent in his eyes. As I continued working on getting Hector to open up, he began telling me bits and pieces about his life before he was adopted by a relative when he was ten. He mentioned doing drugs with his mother, his dad's consistently empty promises to him and his siblings, his father's gang involvement, and how all he knew was the streets. While staff repeatedly asked me, "Why don't you work with a kid that actually wants to be helped?" I clung to my hope for Hector and his future.

After days of pulling him out of class to sit and talk, I walked into the detention center classroom and found Hector quietly studying for his TASC. When I asked what he was doing, he stated, "I'm keeping to myself and behaving like you told me to. Here, I wrote this," and he handed me a sheet with cursive scrawled across the page: "Why have sorrow if life isn't guaranteed live life and help your soul become clean people like to shout and scream but won't open their eyes to see life isn't nothing but a dream until you wake up you won't be able to help yourself succeed so why cry whimp and scream."

For the next couple of weeks, Hector once again demonstrated model resident behavior until he got into an argument with a staff member one morning. A commonly known fact by anyone that knows him, Hector does not like authoritative figures, particularly dominant males. After Hector was "pointed" (a method of the facility's behavior management program that results in a loss of privileges when too many points are accumulated) by a male staff member, the staff instructed Hector to go to his room to spend an hour being disciplined for poor behavior. As I observed on the cameras after the incident, Hector walked a few feet toward his room and then appeared conflicted as he attempted to walk back into the classroom to rejoin the other residents.

Attempting to keep Hector from getting additional residents involved in the situation that was unfolding, the staff member with whom Hector was angry repeatedly held out his arms and shadowed Hector as he continuously tried to maneuver around the staff member back into the classroom.

Hector faked a punch, and the staff member flinched. "You a bitch!" Hector laughed as he faked a second punch. Pacing back and forth for what seemed like an eternity, Hector appeared to battle his urge to hit the staff member and avoid catching a charge for assaulting a public safety official. Finally, Hector snapped and lunged toward the staff member. They went around in circles with arms interlocked three times before wrestling each other to the floor, Hector aimlessly throwing wild punches.

The staff member kicked Hector in the face in the process of trying to get him off of himself, and blood started flowing. Clearly infuriated by the kick to the face, Hector lunged toward the staff member's head and continued throwing wildly aimless punches.

At this point, the staff member rolled over and managed to pin Hector down, leaving him breathless and red-faced until another staff member intervened. Hector was handcuffed, shackled, and led limping to his room.

As a result of his attack on staff, Hector was left in his cell from Friday morning until Monday morning the following week, only allowed out for a five-minute shower each day. Each time I completed a guard tour throughout his time in isolation, Hector would strike up a conversation as quickly as he could before I would pass by his door out of earshot. He became even more grateful for conversation than usual, frequently buzzing into the control room when he knew I was working in the room alone, as the intercom system was intended for emergency use only.

"Yes, Hector?" I would always ask when he buzzed in. His typical responses were, "What you been up to?" and "I'm bored. Will you talk to me?" Always grateful for conversation, Hector would frequently wave staff over to visit him in East Wing, where he was confined, showing them pictures of islands and countries out of a travel destination book that he thought he would like to visit someday.

Several days after the incident with the staff member, Hector shared this poem with me, attempting to convey the conflicting feelings he experienced each time we talked about the importance of making a conscious decision to take a different path:

**Now Corrupted**
Sometimes I sit nd think why did dis world corrupt me
so much people say dey see a difference in me a change
but I cant see it Im stuck in a mindset dat I cant change
people want me to open up but I cant Im not a box Im not
susposed to open up so why keep telling nd yellin its not
gon make a difference people dont change on demand so
whats da difference between me n yu is it dat I wear grey
nd tan yu wear black n blue but we both bleed red nd dats
da truth so why sit here nd act different wen people go an
expose yu but I was here dis whole time tryn tell people
dat dats not da real yu aint no different now yu done hid
behind da lies dat yu cried dats true so why keep asking
god for forgiveness wen dats tha devil nd not you.

The day before Hector's court date, where it was expected that he would be waived from the juvenile into the adult system, I visited with Hector for nearly an hour to once again discuss his post-release plans.

"I want to get out and get my shit straight, so then if I get locked up again, at least I will have all that taken care of. I'm gonna get a crib, a job, all that." We discussed his concerns and his expectation that he will be locked up again in the future. "I don't wanna change and then still end up getting killed. Then what would be the point?" he remarked. "I want to be better, but it's really hard to just change overnight. Plus, even if I change, that doesn't mean everybody else is gonna change too."

Hector and I discussed the paradox that thousands of youth experience throughout the country: Gang affiliation increases one's risk of danger, incarceration, and death, yet leaving the gang also increases one's likelihood of danger, incarceration, and death. "You say you want me to leave the gang, but then you'd be at my funeral, and I'd be looking up at you saying, 'I tried to change, Sam, and look what happened.'"

After talking in circles about these societal issues that are yet to be solved, I reminded Hector to be respectful to the judge in court. "Be smart and safe," I advised him.

"Right, you too." He grinned back as I left.

The following day, Hector was waived to the adult system and transported to the county jail.

Two days after his transport, I received a call from the jail. "Hector?" I asked when I answered the call.

"No, my name's Stuart, but I'm in the jail here with Hector," the caller stated. "Hector told me you may have some housing available."

I smiled to myself as I thought about little Hector sitting in jail yet still watching out for the well-being of the adult men in his unit.

That afternoon, I went to visit Hector at the jail. Because the facility only offered video visitation, I scheduled a visit and proceeded to the visitation room. I dialed in and picked up the phone, waiting for Hector to appear on the screen. Hector answered the video call, immediately breaking out into his big, goofy grin. "What's good?" he asked. "I got bond set at $1,500," he told me happily. "My people's might have me outta here tonight."

"Do you have a plan for what you're going to do once you're

out?" I questioned him, hopeful that he would still be thinking about the list of goals we created together while he was still in the detention center.

"I'm probably just gonna go get fucked up with my boys the first night," he stated, trying to remain nonchalant until he got a reaction out of me.

I gave Hector my best "I care about you, so I want to see you go down the right path" glare as he broke out laughing.

"Nah, I'm going to go get myself enrolled in Central so I can get my TASC," he stated. Hector told me about the other seven men in his unit in the facility. "It's alright in here," he assured me, "I'm just chillin'."

Four hours after I returned home from the visit, an email from the jail's video visitation provider popped up in my inbox. "Hector has invited you to download the new GettingOut Visits app. Visits are only $0.25 per minute. Using an Android or iOS device, you can video visit with your loved one anytime, anywhere!" As Hector never received a visit during the months he spent detained in the juvenile center, I felt both sad and humbled by his excitement over our morning visit and his desire for more attention.

A couple of days later, I was sitting in a symposium at the university I was attending when one of my youth reentry clients, Danny, texted me, "I bailed Hector out, but I don't think he can stay at my crib."

I called Danny, asking to speak with Hector. "Hector, where are you staying tonight?" I questioned.

"I don't know, Sam. Can I stay with you?"

After explaining to Hector that I couldn't have him stay with me but promising that I would attempt to find somewhere else for him to stay, Hector determined that he would stay the night with another boy who had recently been released from the juvenile detention center and lived locally.

The following morning, Hector messaged me at 8:30 a.m., asking if I could drive him to check in with his probation officer at 9:00 a.m. "I'll take you, but you need to start thinking more proactively," I explained as Hector laughed.

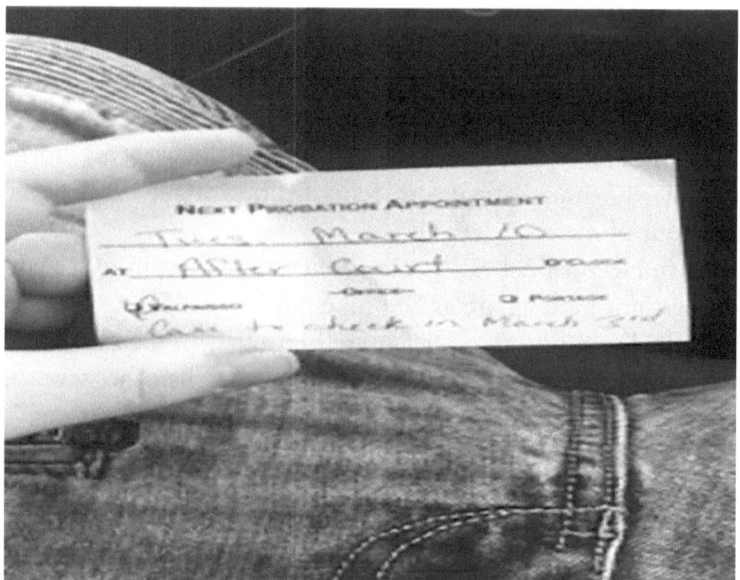

*Taking a picture of Hector's reminder slip for his next probation appointment to decrease the likelihood that he misses the appointment.*

In response to a Facebook post I had created requesting donations of gently used men's clothing for the boys I was working with, a donor reached out and stated that she would like to purchase interview clothes for one of the boys. I drove Hector to a local Salvation Army store, where we planned to meet up with the donor. Appearing lost amidst the racks of dress shirts and pants, Hector poked through the hangers, seeming unsure of what to look for until the donor and I began making recommendations. Completely overwhelmed by the process, Hector simply allowed the donor and me to instruct him on which clothes to put on and then stared at himself in the mirror as we rolled and tucked his pants and shirt sleeves for the next couple of hours. Hector left the store with two pairs of dress pants, three dress shirts, a suit jacket, and his first pair of dress shoes—but most importantly, with a sense of confidence and a desire to secure a job and begin making improvements in his life.

The following weekend, I took Hector to a homeless outreach event that I was helping coordinate at a local church. While Hector was already aware that I would never approve of him wearing his black bandanna, a symbol of his gang, in public, he came running out of the house to my car wearing the bandanna rolled up as a headband. Aware that it would be necessary to pick and choose my battles, especially on a day I was taking him to help with a project he was not explicitly thrilled about, I did not press hard about removing the headband.

When we arrived at the church, Hector met the pastor who, much to Hector's surprise, was also a person of color and very young. The pastor shook hands with Hector and led us down the hallway to the event. As soon as the pastor turned his back to walk down the hallway, Hector swiftly pulled the bandanna off his head and handed it to me behind his back. I swallowed my laughter as I tucked his bandanna into my purse and thought about Hector's surprise when he was not greeted by a white, elderly pastor who knew nothing about gang life or the inner city.

One Saturday morning, a couple of weeks later, I drove to where Hector was staying to pick him up for a local mentoring group session. Hector came walking out of the house, his head facing the ground as he sauntered toward my car. As he drew closer, I pretended not to notice as he attempted to cover his ear-to-ear grin with his hand. He hopped into the front seat, bubbling with excitement as he waited to see my reaction to his new nose piercing. Hector's intense focus on what my reaction to his piercing might be made it impossible to ignore the situation.

"What made you decide to get that?" I asked him, thinking about the extra barriers to employment that he really did not need.

"I don't know. I just wanted it," he responded, attempting to sound nonchalant. "I'm getting a tattoo right here next," he stated, pointing above his left eyebrow while closely eying my face for a reaction.

"What would you get there?" I questioned him.

"Royal with a crown right above it," he responded, indicating a reference to his gang. Hector smiled and seemed to watch my face closely so he could soak up every ounce of my concern and apparent stress.

On my way to pick up Hector for his mentoring group session the following week, I called him to make sure that he would be ready to leave when I arrived. "Be ready in a few minutes," I informed him. "Outside," I texted him when I arrived at the house. After a few minutes of no response, I called his phone instead. No answer. "Hector, I'm here," I texted him again.

Several minutes later, Hector came lounging out of the house. He was walking exasperatingly slow toward my car. As he slid into the front seat, he slowly turned to look at me. Hector mumbled a string of imperceptible words as his eyes closed slowly and opened again halfway.

"Hector, what did you smoke?" I asked loudly, alarmed by his disorientation.

"Nothing," he murmured. "Where are we going?" I thought I heard him mumble.

"We are supposed to be going to mentoring, but I'm not taking you there like this," I stated.

Rather than responding, Hector stared out the windshield, appearing to forget where he was.

"Hector, are you alright?" I asked him, debating whether or not I needed to take him to the hospital. We sat in the driveway for several minutes, after which Hector appeared to become more coherent.

"Come on. We need to go to the group. Danny is meeting us there," Hector explained.

"No, I am not taking you there while you're high," I explained.

"You're going to make me go back inside?" Hector asked, suddenly sounding upset.

"No, we are going to go somewhere and talk," I informed him. With McDonald's being the closest restaurant with a dining room, I drove to McDonald's.

"Come on, Sam. Let me go to the group," Hector continued to complain.

"You knew that we were going to mentoring at eleven o'clock, and you chose to get high this morning, so you aren't going," I responded.

After ordering Hector a McChicken and a chocolate shake, as I was concerned that he had no food at home, we sat and discussed what he wanted for the future and how his decisions were not helping him to achieve his goals.

"Hector, do you know why I am always on you about not smoking and pushing you to apply for jobs and do things to help get you on the right path?" I asked him.

"Because you care about me," he responded quietly as he stared at the table.

"You're right. But me wanting you to do better isn't enough," I explained. "You have to want it for yourself."

"I do, but nobody wants to hire me," Hector stated, sounding defeated as he began eating his sandwich.

As I drove Hector home, he pointed to a pool in the backyard of one of the homes we passed. "I almost drowned in that pool," he stated.

"What happened?" I asked.

"I was riding on the back of a dirt bike with no shoes on, and the exhaust burnt my foot," he explained. "And my mom didn't know I couldn't swim, so she threw me in the pool, but I was really little, so I almost drowned." He laughed the story off, appearing unsure of how to feel about the situation.

A few days later, I picked Hector up at the home where he was staying, as we planned to work on the reentry home recently acquired by my nonprofit organization. As I pulled down the street away from the house, Hector asked sheepishly, "Sam, I hate to bother you, but do you think you could get me something to eat?"

Shocked that he actually asked for something, I pulled into the McDonald's drive-thru. "What are you having?" I asked Hector.

"Umm, a sausage McMuffin," he responded quietly.

"And to drink?"

"Orange juice," he replied cautiously. Hector inhaled the meal in three minutes flat, his mood immediately improving.

When we arrived at the reentry home that we were gutting that day, Hector began tearing out carpet from the bedrooms, clearly enjoying the feeling of being useful. At one point, a neighbor from across the street walked out from his house and stood in the street, appearing to side-eye the house we were working in. Hector tensed up and suggested that we close the front door. "You know, before you started picking me up to do stuff, I was always toting guns," he stated. "But I haven't been lately because I know you would freak out."

*Hector helping to tear carpet out of the bedrooms in the reentry homes.*

After several hours of removing flooring and bathroom appliances, several stakeholders interested in investing in the other reentry home owned by my nonprofit organization came to tour the property. After introducing myself to the investors, I introduced Hector as a participant in the organization's reentry program. He shook hands with each of the investors. As I led the investors through the house, Hector followed quietly behind, soaking in each word and occasionally shaking his head in agreement.

After the tour, one of the stakeholders asked Hector what grade he was in. Shifting from foot to foot, Hector hesitated as he thought about how to answer the question. "Uhh, I'm not in school," he finally responded. "I'm working toward my GED."

The investor, looking slightly concerned, was also unsure of how to respond. Attempting to clarify why such a young person was no longer in school, I explained, "Hector just got out of jail a few weeks ago. He's working to get on the right track now," I explained.

"That's real good then, young man," the investor said, smiling.

"We can get you involved in some of our programs," he stated, making references to several organizations with which he was partnered.

Shaking his head to demonstrate understanding and appreciation, as he usually did when he did not fully understand something, Hector appeared to express interest in the opportunity.

As the investors, Hector, and I gathered in a circle to discuss the next steps before the investors left, the wind picked up. Hector, wearing only a short-sleeve shirt, was bouncing up and down and trying to shrink into his shirt to escape the wind. "Why don't you go inside and grab your jacket," I encouraged him quietly.

Hector took a couple of steps toward the house, then hesitated and came back. "Nah, I'm alright," he stated, clearly not wanting to be excluded from an important conversation that he felt included in.

As the investors continued speaking about the city council and the importance of political power in the community, Hector grasped the opportunity to contribute to the conversation. "You guys probably know my uncle!" he exclaimed.

"Who's your uncle?" one of the investors asked.

"The last mayor out here," he responded.

"Ah yes, we know him," the investors responded, smiling. After asking more about Hector's family and his ties to the community, the investors left.

Intrigued by the fact that Hector had family involved in politics while a majority of his family has been incarcerated numerous times, I inquired more about his uncle.

"Yeah, he isn't the mayor anymore because he was caught stealing money from the city," he stated matter-of-factly. "It was really another guy that did it, but he was still arrested for it," Hector explained. Unsure of whether I should laugh or cry over the fact that this was the time Hector chose to share with the investors, I stopped asking questions for the remainder of the day.

Hector and I were tearing out old tile and scraping flaky paint in the reentry home later that afternoon when I received word that a friend of mine who lived nearby was willing to let Hector sleep on his couch for a couple of weeks while we tried to find him a job locally so that it would be easier for me to transport him to and from work.

I informed Hector, "I found somewhere you can stay."

"When?" Hector questioned as he broke into a big grin.

"Starting tonight, if you want," I responded.

Eyes wide, Hector asked expectantly, "What's my curfew?" seeming to crave the structure and rules that he was anticipating in his new environment.

"It depends," I responded. "If you are thinking you can go out with friends in the streets as long as it is within a certain time frame, then think again."

Hector was smiling ear to ear. Once we were finished up at the house for the day and on our way back home, Hector, who appeared tired and had been riding quietly up to this point, asked, "Can we go and sign up for school tomorrow morning?"

Hector, also determined to improve his situation by obtaining his driver's permit, was texting his friends on Messenger on the phone that I let him borrow later that evening. "Here you go," I stated as I tossed him a Bureau of Motor Vehicles (BMV) manual to study.

"I don't even need to study. I already know this stuff," Hector insisted.

When I informed him that I would not take him to the BMV to take the permit test until he had studied, Hector reluctantly flipped to the practice tests in the back of the manual. "These are easy," Hector adamantly stated as he continued to become confused by the practice questions that I asked him to read aloud and then answer.

As I found Hector glued to his phone each time I turned around to see if he was reading the manual, I decided to begin quizzing him myself. "What is this sign?" I asked him, pointing to a picture of a divided highway sign.

"Oh, uhhhhh, that's a diamond-shaped sign," Hector responded confidently.

Stunned by his response, I glanced over the sign section in the manual, searching for where he had found his answer. Trying my best to hold back laughter, I explained to Hector how the signs were categorized by shape but that he needed to know what each sign signified rather than merely memorizing what the shapes of different signs meant.

After studying the driver's manual, frequently interrupted by Facebook messages, Hector asked if his friend, Danny, another REACH participant, could come hang out in the amenity center downstairs.

"Alright, but only for a little while because it's already late," I responded.

Danny arrived, and we went to the amenity center. While I worked on my laptop, the two boys went straight to the punching bag in the weight room. Five minutes later, Hector came out and ran over to show me his thumb that he was sure he had hurt on the punching bag. I assured him that I thought he was likely to survive.

"Let's play pool, Danny," Hector prodded. "I'll put $40 on it."

"Be careful, Hector," I cautioned. "That's money to get your driver's permit tomorrow."

"Alright, I put $20 on it," Hector conceded.

After their pool game, Hector and Danny announced that they needed to go to the gas station to get something to drink. Suspicious, I asked Hector if he was planning to go to the gas station and smoke.

"No, no," Hector assured me, shaking his head.

"Danny?" I questioned. "Are you guys trying to go out and smoke?"

Danny, known to be a terrible liar, glanced down for a short time before he couldn't hold back a grin any longer. "I ain't gonna lie. We were gonna smoke just a little," Danny finally stated.

"No, you can't go out," I informed the boys.

Danny and Hector settled for another game of ping-pong and then, twenty minutes later, stated that they needed to go out to Danny's car to get a pair of shorts for Hector to work out in.

"Are you planning to go out and smoke?" I questioned the two boys.

"No, we legit need to get Hector some shorts out of my car," Danny stated.

"Alright, I'll come with you," I decided.

"Mama Sam," Hector sighed as the three of us walked toward the door.

As we walked outside, Danny and Hector hung back slightly behind me. I turned around to find Hector smoking a cigarette.

"Hector, are you kidding? You don't need that," I exclaimed. A few steps later, I caught a whiff of marijuana and quickly noted Hector's lit cigarette, and Danny's body turned away from me. "Danny, you think I can't smell that?" I asked harshly, as he quickly turned around with a blunt in his hand. "Both of you put those out now," I demanded. After I ordered Danny to leave all paraphernalia in his car, I walked both boys back into the amenity center.

While Hector and Danny went back to the gym, I pretended to work on my computer as I monitored them out of the corner of my eye. A couple of minutes later, I noticed Hector standing in the middle of the gym, peeking out the glass window at me. Frustrated, I walked quickly toward the weight room as Hector turned and said something to Danny, and Danny leaped up from the machine he was sitting at out of view of the window.

As soon as I opened the door of the weight room, I could smell marijuana. Determined to teach a lesson rather than merely yell, I informed Danny and Hector of the many potential negative impacts of smoking in such a public place.

"That's why we were trying to go out, so we could avoid smoking here," Danny and Hector explained. I indicated that it was time for Danny to leave.

"So what you wanna do, man? You coming with?" Danny asked Hector.

Hector, looking torn, glanced at me. "You can go with him, but you can't come back here after," I told him. Hector looked back and forth from Danny to me before stating, "I need her to take me to do stuff in the morning," to Danny.

Looking halfway ashamed, Danny said lowly, "Alright, I guess I'm gonna head out then."

"Go home and be smart, Danny. Don't go out tonight. It's already late," I warned him.

Once Danny walked out the door, Hector looked sheepishly at me, dragging his feet as he followed me back down the stairs. Seeming to hold his breath, waiting to hear what I would say, Hector sat down and began explaining himself in a much more child-like voice than he had used just two minutes prior while talking with his friend.

The following morning, determined to get Hector enrolled in GED classes, we went to the local alternative school, which offers both GED classes and alternative high school courses. We approached the front desk as the secretary asked how she could help us.

Glancing at Hector, who appeared unsure of how to respond, I stated, "We need to get him enrolled in GED classes."

"Alright, how old are you?" the woman asked Hector.

"Seventeen," he responded.

"What is the highest grade level you completed?" she questioned.

"I dropped out in eighth grade," he stated.

"So you only completed seventh grade," she said, more to herself than to us.

"Well, you need an exit interview from your last school before we can get you signed up for GED here," she explained.

"What would the process be like if he took normal high school classes here instead?" I asked.

The woman spoke with another staff member and then came back to inform us that it would take at least three years for Hector to earn enough credits to graduate. Clearly feeling defeated and frustrated, Hector accepted the woman's business card and walked out of the office. On our way back to the car, he noticed one of his old friends being dropped off at the facility.

"What up, G?" Hector shouted to the boy. The two shook hands and slapped each other on the back. "I'm about to start coming here!" Hector shouted to the boy as he continued walking to the car. "See you soon, man!"

As we made calls to former juvenile facilities Hector had been detained at to secure documentation required by the school to enroll in GED courses, I drove to the BMV so Hector could take his driver's permit test. One of the BMV staff called our number and asked how she could help us.

"He needs to take a driver's permit test," I stated.

"Alright, how old are you?" she asked Hector.

"Seventeen," he responded.

"We need a parent or guardian to come with you then," she stated.

"Here are the authorization papers," I stated as I slid her the form that I had completed with his legal guardian the night before.

"Alright, you're set up on computer four," she informed Hector.

"If you fail the exam, you don't need to tell us. You can just come back the next day and try again."

"Thank you," Hector said gruffly as he stood up and began walking toward the computers.

"Go slow!" I called out to Hector as he glanced back over his shoulder and grinned.

Fifteen minutes later, Hector turned around at the computer and shrugged at me. "I don't know what happened," he called out as I walked toward him. "It just kicked me off. I think I passed, though," he stated.

"I guess we'll ask if they can check at the desk," I responded.

When our new number was called and another staff member checked his exam results, she explained, "The computer kicks you off the exam if you miss too many."

"So I didn't pass?" Hector questioned.

"No. It looks like you missed too many questions on the sign portion," she stated.

"Alright, thank you," Hector stated, appearing frustrated as he began walking out of the building.

"It's alright. A lot of people fail the test on their first try," I assured him. "At least now we know that you definitely need to study the signs better before you take it again."

"Man, I really thought I did good," he sighed.

While preparing to go meet a donor at the reentry house later in the week, Hector persistently asked if he could go outside and 'smoke a square.'

"Nope, you don't need one," I responded.

Hector appeared slightly annoyed yet simultaneously pleased that someone was watching out for him.

On the way to the reentry house, I quizzed Hector on each road sign we passed. Once we arrived at the house, Hector helped unload the toilet and vanity being donated and happily trailed behind the donors as they toured the home. As we passed the gas station at the corner of the street when we left the reentry house for the day, Hector reminisced about the time he was almost shot at the gas station while attempting to protect his mother as she stumbled around, drunkenly instigating fights.

*Hector helping with the rehabilitation of the Community Change Center's reentry homes.*

I picked Hector up for his court hearing the following Wednesday at 8:05 a.m., questioning whether he was planning to wear the white slides he had on his feet into the court hearing. When we arrived at the third floor of the courthouse and sat on the bench to wait for the hearings to begin, Hector suddenly threw his head down into his hands. "Fuck," he moaned quietly.

"What's wrong?" I asked.

"I think I was supposed to call my attorney, but I forgot," Hector complained.

"Who is your public defender?" I asked.

"I don't remember," Hector stated miserably as he cautiously glanced at me, seeming both amused and afraid of what my reaction may be to his response.

"Well, hopefully, your attorney will find you before the hearing," I half-heartedly attempted to reassure him, while simultaneously chastising him for his last-minute preparations for such a critical event.

As the respondents who were brought to court in the custody of the county jail had to have their cases heard first by the judge, Hector and I were forced to wait for his hearing. After three hours of tensely waiting for Hector's name to be called, the judge called his name, and he sauntered up to the front of the courtroom. "Your honor, I would like to request additional time to review this case. I would like to request a continuance," Hector's public defender, who had known Hector before Hector knew him, announced.

"Alright, you are ordered to appear on April 28th at 9:00 a.m.," the court recorder announced to Hector.

After court, Hector determined that he would like to study to retake his driver's permit test. After two to three hours of studying and passing two online practice tests, Hector insisted that he was ready to go to the BMV and retake his permit test.

"Do you think I'll pass?" he constantly asked as we prepared to head to the BMV. After grabbing a ticket at the front desk, we sat and waited for our number to be called. Hector anxiously jiggled his leg as he sat next to me, awaiting to take the test. "I'm gonna be pissed if I don't pass," he stated. "If I don't pass, just make me walk home," he said.

Once we had checked in, I reminded Hector to read all the questions and answers slowly before selecting an answer. He grinned quickly over his shoulder as he approached computer one, where his test was set up.

After twenty minutes, I was practically holding my breath as I waited for Hector to either pass the test or be kicked off the exam for missing too many questions. Finally, he turned around and defeatedly shook his head at me. Recognizing his disappointment, I quickly approached him and reminded him that it takes a lot of people multiple attempts to pass the test.

"I'm so fucking pissed," Hector repeated as we exited the BMV. "I need to fight somebody," he demanded.

"You can go use the punching bag," I stated flatly.

"No, it isn't the same," Hector insisted. "I'm so pissed. Matter of fact, just make me walk home," he stated as he opened the car door from the inside.

"Shut the door, Hector," I demanded. "You're fine. We can try it again tomorrow."

Later in the evening, I was preparing dinner for Hector and several of my friends while Hector played YouTube videos on the television and called friends on Facebook Messenger. I listened quietly as Hector argued over the phone. When he hung up, I cautiously asked him what was wrong.

"My mom wants to keep blowing up my phone," he responded.

"What's wrong with her wanting to check in on you?" I asked.

"Because she wants to talk shit to all her friends like she's done all this shit for me my whole life when really she was never even around!" he exclaimed. "I took care of it. I just had to make a call to the Kings," he explained nonchalantly.

Concerned about how Hector might respond if I pressed further, I left the conversation alone.

"Can I have some water?" Hector asked me.

Silently, I filled a glass with water and handed it to him. After digging around in his backpack, Hector retreated to the bathroom with the glass of water in his hand. As I noticed Hector disappear into the bathroom, I suddenly felt that something was not right. Standing outside the door, I thought through every worst-case scenario that could be occurring inside. As I prepared to knock on the door and see what he was doing, Hector exited the bathroom with half a glass of water left. Thinking he might have been smoking marijuana in the bathroom, I walked into the room but detected no scent.

I walked back into the kitchen and observed Hector and his behaviors for several minutes as I continued preparing dinner. Within ten minutes, Hector was swaying back and forth with the music, and I noted his dilated pupils. "What did you take?" I asked him.

"What do you mean, Sam?" Hector asked, seeming to attempt to sound innocent. "I didn't take anything," he declared.

I continued to observe as he appeared to become more and more relaxed and unaware of his surroundings. Talking on Facebook Messenger, Hector asked a friend, "You finna slide through, bro? Mothafucka is bored as hell."

Several minutes later, Hector stated that he was going downstairs to work out in the weight room.

"Hector, where are you going?" I asked him as he exited the apartment.

"Downstairs," he responded nonchalantly as he prepared to head down the stairs.

"Come here," I demanded.

Walking slowly with a grin on his face, Hector approached me.

"What, Sam?" he asked.

"What did you take?" I asked him again. "I want to know if you are alright."

"Fine, I took two Xans," he answered.

"Why did you do that?" I questioned him.

"Because everybody is really testing me tonight," he responded.

"Can you tell me what made you upset?" I encouraged.

"I don't talk about my feelings," he stated.

"Sometimes that's what you have to do so that you don't have to bottle it all up until you feel like you need to take Xanax to deal with life," I stated.

"I don't talk about my feelings," Hector stated adamantly.

I followed him downstairs, confident that we could have an emotional breakthrough if I could just convince Hector to recognize the link between what made him upset and his decision to use prescription drugs.

"C'mon, Sam, let's play pool," Hector prompted, attempting to change the conversation when we arrived at the amenity center downstairs. After nearly an hour of playing pool while discussing the pros and cons of talking through feelings, Hector acknowledged, "Sam, you look so stressed."

"Gee, I wonder why," I remarked.

"I really appreciate you, Sam," Hector sincerely stated as he held out his arms for a hug.

"I want you to be safe, Hector," I explained. "I need you to give me the rest of the Xanax."

Hector's mouth dropped open in disbelief. After contemplating methods for avoiding the surrender of the pills, Hector sighed. "Fine," he stated as he handed me a pocketful of pills.

"Turn your pockets inside out," I instructed him.

Three more pills fell onto the ground. Hector stared at the pile of pills in my hand. "You're real lucky, Sam," he stated. "I wouldn't just do that for anybody."

Hector called me while I was at the office working one morning. "I'm at the door. Come let me in," he stated when I answered the phone. "I just stopped by to say hi before my interview," he explained as he ran back to his sister's car.

"You have forty-five minutes before the interview, and Chili's is right down the street!" I laughed.

"I know, but it might take a while to get there," Hector responded.

"Alright, you can come back after the interview and fill out your Qdoba application," I said.

"Alright, be safe!" Hector yelled as he hopped into the waiting car.

An hour later, Hector called again, informing me that he was outside the office. While his little sisters, who had driven him to the interview, went to play pool and ping-pong in the lower level of the office, I helped Hector complete the job application.

"What are two of your favorite Qdoba menu items?" one of the questions asked.

"I don't know. I've never even been to Qdoba!" Hector exploded, throwing himself back on the couch. "Chorizo."

"I don't see chorizo on the online menu. Put a chicken bowl," I replied.

"Alright, what else?" Hector asked after writing his first favorite menu item.

"Uh, Hector. We're gonna have to change that," I said as I glanced over his application responses up to that point. "Chicken bowel" was written across the first line of the "favorite menu items" question. Hector nervously laughed as I instructed him to rewrite the word, although it was unclear to me whether or not he knew what the issue was.

While on my way to work one Friday afternoon, Hector called to inform me that his friend was having a party and renting out a hotel room that night. "You can pick me up afterwards if you want," he stated. Planning to pick him up from the party once I was off work, I checked my messages halfway through my shift. "I'm staying out here tonight," Hector had said, following the message with a thumbs-up emoji. At the end of my shift, I saw that Hector had texted me, "Can yu pick me up," followed by an address to a local trailer park. I picked Hector up, and he immediately asked if we could stop and get a sandwich.

"Why did you decide you wanted to be picked up?" I asked.

"My friend's dad was trippin', and I didn't want to deal with it," he responded. I decided not to press any further, already impressed that he had made the choice to remove himself from the situation as things began amping up at his friend's house.

After begging me for weeks to let him join one of my visits with Elias, another boy involved in the REACH program, in the county jail, I let Hector sit in on an online visit with him. When Elias's face appeared on the screen, Hector observed his new haircut.

"Damn, nigga, they fucked yo shit up!" Hector cried.

Elias gave a half-grin as he ran his hand over his freshly cut hair.

"It looks fine, Elias," I assured him.

"Yeah, I'm alright with it," Elias replied.

"G, I've been telling all the boys they need to be callin' you, man, because now you're locked up, and they really be doin' you like that," Hector ranted. "Hey, bro, lemme give you my number so you can call me."

As he began rambling about drama in the outside world, I reminded Hector that Elias was determined to stay on a straight path once he got out. I told Elias that Hector was starting GED classes in April and had been completing job applications and interviews in an attempt to redirect both boys.

"Yeah, bro, I'm starting school soon," Hector proudly stated after Elias spoke about his own desire to get into GED classes once he was released from jail. Suddenly the "1 minute remaining" warning flashed across the screen.

"Keep your head up, Elias. You're doing good," I assured him.

"Hey, bro, I love you!" Hector practically shouted as the visit ended.

Throughout the day, Hector answered numerous phone calls from friends. "Bro, you gotta get the honey-colored stuff, or they're gonna know you tampered with it," he stated on one call. "I'll slide through later, and we can just go get it," he said on another.

As I drove him to his auntie's house later in the afternoon, I lectured him about the importance of not involving himself with others who do, sell, or carry drugs, as he could get himself into trouble simply by associating with them.

"I'm low-key, Sam. Even if they got busted, I won't," he explained.

We discussed his theory in-depth, and I could see him processing the conversation. "You have people to take care of you, Hector. I don't want to see you get locked up for years before you learn that you need to stop doing this stuff and endangering yourself and your freedom."

"I know, Sam. I'm trying," he stated, sounding somewhat

defeated and tired. When I dropped Hector off, he gave me a hug, and I reminded him to be smart and safe.

At 12:30 a.m., Danny, another boy in the REACH program, texted me. "Aye. Me n Hector r together n we out in da city." A couple of minutes later, Hector called off Danny's phone. "We're in the city and got a hotel room for the night," he said.

"Why are you two out in the city?" I pressed.

"Don't trip. We're safe. I'll be back your way tomorrow," Hector responded.

"Be careful," I warned before he hung up.

Hector's legal guardian texted me the following day, "Can you call me please." As soon as she answered, I could hear the exhaustion in her voice. "Can you pick up Hector's stuff tomorrow? I have to protect my girls. I've tried to do everything for him, but he keeps going back to all this gang shit. He brought a gun in my house, and I think he knows that I know. And he brought one of his friends over that he knows isn't allowed over here. I told him that his friend had to leave, and he said he was leaving too."

The following morning, I went to pick up Hector's belongings. One backpack and a trash bag later, he was moved out of his aunt's house. I went to pick up Hector for his dentist appointment next. During the drive to the dentist, Hector asked, "Can you drop me off at my crib after?"

"Which one?" I asked.

"My auntie's," he responded.

"Hector, your aunt called me last night to come pick up your stuff. She's tired, and she has to protect your sisters from all the dangerous things that you are wrapped up in," I tried to explain.

Hector sat in silence for a second. "She doesn't want me back there?" he questioned.

"I know that she wants you to stay there, but she can't have you staying there when you are out doing the things you've been doing," I tried to explain.

Hector sat in silence a while longer. "Fuck them two-faced ass bitches," he finally stated.

"She knew where I was going the other night, and now she want to lie on me," he stated angrily, trying to hide how deeply hurt he was feeling.

We pulled up at the dentist's office. "Man, I really don't wanna do this shit. It's gonna hurt," Hector complained. Once he was checked in and called back to a room, Hector was seated in the chair with the dentist reading over his chart.

"We definitely are not going to get all this work done in one hour," the dentist stated.

Hector looked at me hopefully. "Want to just reschedule?" he asked.

"How much of it can we get done today?" I asked the dentist.

"He needs seven fillings," the dentist responded.

"We can get two or three of them done today."

"That'll work, thank you," I responded.

"Would you like silver or white fillings?" the dentist questioned.

"Do you have gold?" Hector asked.

I informed the dentist that white would do.

"Do you know the Wi-Fi password here?" Hector asked the dentist.

After pausing to make sure he heard correctly, the dentist informed Hector that he was the wrong person to ask about the password. One hour and three white fillings later, Hector walked out of the office, complaining about his half-numb smile.

After lunch that day, Hector asked to stay with a friend of his for the night so he could go to work with him the following day. Hesitant to let him stay with a friend I did not know but hoping he truly would gain some work experience and life skills, I consented.

"Thanks, ma. It will be good for me, I promise," Hector assured me. Hector continued staying with his friend, assuring me daily that they were working on cars and that he was learning a lot.

One of Hector's relatives texted me a couple of weeks later. "Can you call me?" She asked if I had heard from Hector.

"I've been checking in with him every day but haven't heard from him since yesterday evening," I responded.

She proceeded to tell me what she had found out from others around town, including the drugs and guns being dealt out of the house where he was staying. Both livid and concerned, I searched through Hector's social media, discovering pictures of him with firearms and conversations asking for and selling pills. Throughout his conversations, Hector frequently introduced himself as a "king," informing people that his "pops is a king" and so is he.

At 1:30 a.m., Hector messaged me. "Aye my phone broke so I

dont have one my bad ma I'm ok I'm jus using my brothas until da morning ma n den I should have a new one."

When I read the message later that morning, I warned Hector that everything he had been doing would eventually catch up to him and that he was on the same path that he was on before he was locked up last time. I then reminded him of the people in his corner who want to help him get on the right track and be successful.

Hector responded, "Y is yu mad dats all yu gotta say ma den I'll accept dat n will have to move on with my life thanks ma foreverything yu have done for me I appreciate it I really do n thanks for giving me money n a place to stay ma if I made yu mad I'm sorry buh I'll still b around tryna do my best ma to prove to yall dat I ain't gonna fail like yall think I am buh good night sorry for waking yu up ma."

Once again, I reminded Hector that I wanted what was best for him and knew that where he was staying was not what was best, and once again, Hector assured me that he was in the right place.

I picked Hector up for a probation appointment at eight on Wednesday morning. He came sauntering out of the trailer he had stayed at the night prior, rubbing his eyes and yawning as he slid into the passenger seat.

"Didn't sleep last night?" I asked.

"I did, but I'm just exhausted," he stated as he pulled his hood up, laid his head back, and shut his eyes.

I waited several minutes before launching into the conversation that I could tell he was trying to avoid. "So what's been going on, Hector?" I asked.

"Man, all these motherfuckers be on my back," he remarked. "My uncs called me up yesterday talkin' about why I sent his daughter some message, but how did I send her a message if I've had all them blocked on my shit for weeks?"

I listened in silence as Hector ranted. Once he stopped, he grew silent and laid his head back again. "You know how I told you the other day that there are lots of people who know what you've been up to the past few weeks?" I asked him.

Hector glanced sideways at me. "I'm not saying these things to try and corner you. I'm telling you that I've seen you with the guns and trying to sell drugs. You don't need to try to think about how to deny it because I've already seen it, and I want to have a conversation about it," I stated.

Hector's eyes focused on mine for the first time that morning, and I was unsure if he was about to explode in anger or was holding back tears. He stared at me for a minute, shook his head slightly, and turned his head again to stare out the window. "That wasn't my gun, Sam," he finally replied.

"Hector, the point here is not whether or not the gun was yours. The point is that guns are both dangerous and will violate your probation if you are seen with them, which obviously you are because I know about it," I explained. "Why are you selling pills, Hector?" I asked next. "You have multiple people literally begging you to stop doing what you're doing and to just come stay with them so they can take care of you. Why do you feel the need to sell drugs?"

"I ain't finna be out here broke," Hector replied.

"Well, you're on the path to being back in jail," I warned.

"So? There ain't nothing out here for me anyway," he stated.

"Are you sad about your dad?" I asked as Hector's father had recently been sent back to jail in another state.

"Fuck that nigga," he responded, clearly not wanting to discuss the topic further.

When I dropped Hector off after his probation appointment, he turned to hug me. "If you want to pick me up Friday, we could do more job apps and whatever other shit you want me to do," he stated as he slid out of the car.

A couple of weeks later, Hector came to pick up some of the clothes he had left with me to keep safe, as it is difficult to avoid losing belongings while couch surfing. While he usually asked how I'd been doing when we met up, he simply walked in silence. Finally, I asked what he'd been up to.

"Oh, just hanging out with my family," he responded.

"Which family?" I asked.

"My girl and my kid," he replied, attempting to hold back a grin.

"Your kid?" I asked.

"Yep, my girl is twenty-eight," he responded, glancing at me sideways, still holding back a smile as he gauged my reaction.

"Hector, you know that's illegal, right?" I questioned.

"How?" he asked.

I explained as we walked toward the car he had arrived in. "You didn't drive here, did you?" I pressed.

"Yeah, why wouldn't I?" he asked, seeming to purposefully push all my buttons.

"You don't have a license," I replied, no longer trying to hide my frustration. Rather than giving me a hug as he usually does, Hector parted ways with me in the middle of the parking lot.

Sensing that he did not want me to approach the car, I watched him slide into the passenger seat as I walked away. Later that evening, I sent Hector a message to remind him of his dentist appointment the following morning.

"Ite," he replied.

I asked Hector where he would be the following morning to be picked up, but he did not respond for the rest of the night.

The following morning, Hector texted me at 9:00 a.m., two hours before his appointment. "I'm jus gonna reschedule it," he texted.

I immediately called him. "You cannot cancel this appointment two hours before," I informed him. "It's been scheduled for a month."

"Well, I gotta go with my girl to Chicago today to see if there's a baby or an egg in there or some shit," he stammered.

"Hector, if you do not come to this appointment today, I'm not scheduling another," I stated.

"Why are you mad?" he complained.

"Because you need to be at your appointment today," I responded. I heard a grown woman's voice in the background.

"You're not going," she whispered loudly.

"Hector, I can hear her in the background telling you that you're not coming. You need to let me pick you up for your appointment, or you're not going to get your cavities filled."

Hector was silent until I heard the woman loudly state again, "Tell her you're not going!"

"I'm about to flip out. I'm on the phone!" Hector yelled at her.

"Alright, well, if the girl you are staying with wants to start making decisions for you and making sure you get everywhere, then that's fine," I conceded. I heard her pipe back up in the background.

"I will make sure he gets to probation and shit because I have to go there too," she retorted in the direction of the phone. "And you need to get your social security card and all that paperwork from her too!" she yelled at him.

"I want you to know that you're making bad decisions," I warned Hector.

"Why do all you guys keep calling me to tell me that?" he exclaimed, referring to his family and me.

"Because you are. You shouldn't be there," I responded.

After several months without hearing from Hector, his picture once again appeared on my Telmate account when I logged in to visit with another boy who had been waived from the juvenile to the adult system and was now serving time in the local jail. After a quick search in the recent bookings tab of the Sheriff Department's website, I knew Hector had been arrested for (1) driving without a license and (2) driving while impaired. I sent him a quick message while waiting for my visit to begin.

"Are you ok? Let me know if you want to visit."

"Yeah if you want to," he replied back that afternoon.

When we had our virtual visit later that week, I asked Hector what had happened.

"Well, see, it was some dumb shit. They're gonna have to let me out soon 'cause I didn't do nothin'!" Hector exclaimed.

"Driving while you're high is pretty dangerous," I reminded him. "You risk hurting or killing other people and yourself."

Hector grew quiet for a second before responding, "I mean, I guess, but nobody got hurt."

"You were fortunate this time," I told him. "Now you need to act right in there so you can get out and have another chance to go back to school and work toward all the goals we talked about before."

A few weeks later, Hector went to court and reported back that he "fired" his public defender. As the weeks went on and his family never hired the private attorney Hector claimed they had promised him, Hector seemed to grow more and more defeated. Several months later, Hector called me one day and excitedly told me that he was going to be released at his next court hearing.

On the day of the hearing, I awaited his happy phone call telling me that he was out. However, the following day, Hector called from inside the jail to say he didn't know why they had decided to simply continue his hearing for a few more months. "I don't care anymore," Hector exclaimed one day. "I'm finna go crazy in this bitch, I don't care what happens."

I reminded Hector that any felonies he accrued while incarcerated would follow him for the rest of his life.

"Sam, no, it's gonna be fine. I'll just move to Illinois once I finally get out," he explained.

"What will moving to Illinois do for you?" I asked him, part of me dreading his response.

"I don't have any felonies there," he stated matter-of-factly.

At that moment, I was reminded of the horrific reality that a majority of people trapped within our American justice system have little to no knowledge of the processes they are experiencing and do not understand the decisions being made regarding their lives. Although a majority of people incarcerated in America have done something illegal, sometimes several somethings, to result in their incarceration, it often seems as if they are puppets in their own lives—simply fighting to survive while the more powerful actors determine what their fates shall be.

By the time Hector's next court hearing came, he seemed to have come to this realization as well. A few days after his hearing passed without a phone call, I became concerned that he had received bad news at court and acted out, resulting in him being put in "the hole," or solitary confinement within the jail. I logged into Telmate to schedule a virtual visit. However, Hector was no longer listed on the jail's roster. Confused and somewhat concerned, I waited a few more days to see if he would call. When I still had not received word from him, I finally checked the DOC website for his name. Sure enough, the judge had sent him to prison rather than releasing him at his last hearing. Angry toward the system but relieved to know where he was, I waited for a phone call.

When Hector did call a couple of weeks later, I reminded him that he was eighteen years old in a facility with men much older than him and encouraged him to lie low.

"Nah, Sam, don't worry," he stated. "Everyone in my pod is cool as hell."

Over the following six months he was incarcerated in the prison, Hector and I discussed his plans and goals he wanted to work toward upon his release.

"Well, I'm gonna get out and save up enough money to get an apartment during my first week," he stated excitedly one day.

Humored, saddened, and concerned about the reality check I knew he would receive once he started working and encountering bills in the adult world, I talked through potential job opportunities and interests with him. When his release date in July finally came, Hector excitedly called me from an unknown phone number. "I already checked in at probation, and I'm on my way to the beach to chill for the day!" Hector shouted. "I'll be there for the GED classes tomorrow, though!"

The following day, I sent Hector a message asking him to let me know where he would be at 5:00 p.m. so I could pick him up for his class if he didn't have a ride.

"I'll try to make it," he responded.

I didn't hear from Hector for several months until one day, he sent me a message on Facebook. I asked him if he was ready to join the class, to which he asked whether I was the only teacher. "Are you afraid you're going to get in trouble or what?" I asked him.

"Oh you must not have heard," he replied. "I got a warrant."

I explained to Hector that his punishment would be lesser if he turned himself in. "No I gotta do some good stuff and show them that I'm trying to do better before I turn myself in. You know since I violated, I'm gonna serve some years in prison once I get caught," he responded.

I didn't hear from Hector for the next several weeks and eventually saw him pop up on the local jail roster just four days before Christmas. Several weeks passed, and seeing Hector's name on the roster day in and day out was gnawing at me. Finally, I encountered one of the chaplains from the jail at a community meeting and asked him if he would talk with Hector just to provide him some support while he was incarcerated there. The chaplain assured me that one of his caseworkers in the jail would follow up with Hector.

A few days later, one of the case managers from the jail sent me an email stating that Hector was in disciplinary, so she would be unable to talk with him until he was put back into the general population. Shocked by the fact that Hector was unable to receive therapeutic or supportive services when I knew he needed them most, and with the understanding that he behaved worse when he felt disrespected and out of control rather than protected and loved, I asked if I could come to the jail for an in-person visit with Hector. After explaining that I believed Hector's behavior would improve if I were able to provide him with some support and that I was hoping to talk with him about potentially trying to get him referred to our county's mental health court, I was permitted to schedule a visit with Hector.

When I arrived at the jail on the scheduled day for my visit with Hector, I picked up the phone next to the tinted-glass window and told the jail officer who I was there to visit.

"Are you an officer?" he asked me.

"No, I'm a social worker. The jail's case manager told me she would let you know that I was coming to see Hector today."

The commander paused and asked me to give him a minute to make some calls. Eventually, I was permitted to walk through the metal detector and enter a four-by-four square foot room with a phone and a plexiglass window. "We'll bring him right out," the officers informed me. Approximately ten minutes went by when I saw Hector and a correctional officer arrive at the locked door on the other side of the plexiglass. Hector peered in through the window of the door and burst out in a giant grin and started laughing when he saw me sitting there. He shook his head as he smiled and was permitted to enter the room and sit down on the other side of the glass.

"How are you doing?" I asked him.

"Man, I'm fucking tired of this place," Hector said as he shook his head again. "Did you hear I'm gonna be a dad?" he asked, searching my eyes for my reaction to his news. Thinking about all the times I had warned Hector against having a baby while he was so young and especially against having a baby with someone who was not the right person for him, I told him congratulations.

"My son is the biggest reason I need to get out of here and start getting my shit together," Hector stated, sounding more serious than I had heard him before. Hector talked for the next hour about how when he had been out on pretrial, he had been trying to comply with all the mandated services and was working full-time at a junkyard, but then he had a difficult time making it to all of his appointments so he "went on the run."

With the knowledge that Hector struggled not only with a slight cognitive delay but also with his mental health, I explained to him what problem-solving courts were and what the benefits would be if we got him into the local mental health court. "If you complete the program successfully, you'll benefit from the services they provide, and your charge could be dismissed," I explained.

"Will it get me out of here quicker?" Hector asked.

"Probably so. But you have to have a psychological evaluation done, which will determine whether you do have a mental health diagnosis," I explained. "Remind me, do you have any diagnoses already, like depression, anxiety, anything like that?" I asked him.

"Nope, nothing. I mean, I got ADHD," Hector replied, shrugging. Forty-five minutes into our conversation, Hector disclosed that he was currently being held in solitary confinement for "going off" on the jail staff the week prior.

"What happened?" I asked.

Hector went on to explain that staff accused him of being drunk, which he claimed he was not, so he got angry with them and eventually was tased multiple times and put into "the hole" for an unknown amount of time. I asked Hector about the coping skills we had worked on together years before, and I recommended that he think about his son the next time he starts to get angry. "But it's my bipolar depression!" Hector exclaimed.

"I'm sorry. What did you just say?" I asked in disbelief. "What about an hour ago when I was asking you if you had any mental health diagnoses? You didn't mention that."

Hector grinned, starting to understand the miscommunication. "Well, I didn't know what you meant!" he exclaimed as he laughed.

Hector's referral and acceptance into the local mental health court was denied, resulting in Hector remaining in jail while his attorney worked on his case.

While Hector's story is far from over, it provides a great example of the deep desire within many justice-involved individuals to get their lives on the right track, yet they often face so many barriers to housing, employment, social capital, and so on that it can seem infinitely easier to retreat back to the lifestyle they already know.

# CHAPTER 2

# DAVID

While I was still a relatively new staff member at the detention center, a new intake, David, was arrested and brought to the facility. David was a tall, well-built, sandy blond seventeen-year-old with a friendly smile that never failed to draw the attention of female residents at the center. Everyone at the facility liked David, as he rarely caused issues and went out of his way to watch out for other residents and to be helpful to staff. David had a great sense of humor and was consistently nonchalant, often choosing to laugh off situations that occurred within the facility.

The first time I encountered David, he had just finished completing his intake paperwork upon being arrested and brought to the facility and typically would have been allowed to join the other residents in the Multipurpose Room of the facility. However, due to his behavior the previous time he was incarcerated in the center, he was informed that he had to serve the suspension, or twenty-four hours in his room, that he had not served during his last facility stay. Infuriated and still under the influence of the drugs that had led to his arrest, David swung and knocked the water jug that was sitting on a cart flying into the wall. David was immediately physically restrained and placed in his cell for the next twenty-four hours to serve the suspension.

Two days later, I was back at work and assigned to work on the wing with the older youth, where David was housed. With the knowledge that David had been angry enough to smack the water jug into the wall two days prior, I was preparing myself to deal with an angry and potentially violent resident. When I entered the wing, I located him and introduced myself. He smiled and introduced himself as well. Although David did not disclose much about himself, he was very pleasant and easy to talk with. Due to his history of mental illness, near overdoses, suicide attempts, and the deep scars running across his left arm, the court ordered David to several months in the facility in an attempt to protect him from himself. Never causing any significant issues within the facility, all staff members agreed that David was extremely likable. Toward the end of one of his stays in the facility, I asked David's advice on the nonprofit organization that I was working to create in order to work with older youth coming out of the detention center so that they did not continue to re-offend and find themselves incarcerated over and over again. David provided me with his input, and we often talked about the program until he was released from the facility.

A few months later, I walked into work to discover that David had been arrested again. "What happened?" I inquired when I saw him sitting watching television on the wing that afternoon.

"Probation thinks I gave a dirty drug screen, but I'm clean. It's a false positive, but now I'm stuck here for the weekend, and I'm pissed because I was supposed to go to a party tonight." But, as was David's nature, he was still calm and polite, even as he shared his frustrations with me. He informed me that he had obtained a job and was doing well "on the outs." As I walked off the wing toward the end of the night, David called out, "Hey, Sam, did you start that program you told me about yet?"

"Not yet. It should be started up in the fall," I told him excitedly.

"You should add me on Snapchat," he replied.

I laughed, as social media contact between staff and former residents was strictly forbidden. "Sorry, that's not how this works, David," I chuckled.

The following Monday, David was released from the detention center when the juvenile probation department concluded that the drug screen results had, in fact, yielded a false positive.

Several months later, I was visiting my parents' small lake house one weekend when one of my former co-workers from the detention center came to visit. We were floating around in the lake as I shared with him my excitement to start up my reentry program at the detention center in a few weeks.

"David has been asking about it," I told him. "I think it will be really helpful for older kids like him."

My co-worker's eyes opened wide for a second, and I asked him what was wrong.

"You didn't hear?" he asked. "David died."

My heart dropped, and my body froze. I thought he was joking. "What?" I said in disbelief.

"He overdosed on heroin and died at the hospital. The people he got high with basically dumped him outside the hospital and took off," he stated.

My head spun. "Did you start that program you told me about yet?" played in my head on repeat for weeks as I pictured David's kind face, his scarred wrists, and the ugly disease to which he lost his battle.

# CHAPTER 3

# JOSE

I remember looking through the one-sided glass from the control room to the reception center, seeing a boy, no taller than 5'2", slumped in a chair, with a scowl and a look of annoyance across his face as the transporting police officer completed the affidavit paperwork with a detention officer. Another officer took the boy back into the intake room to complete his paperwork, where the boy stated, "I'm not sure how many pills I took this morning. Probably like twenty."

The intake officer shared this information with the supervisor, who called the facility nurse and determined that the boy needed to be evaluated in the emergency room to ensure that he was not going to overdose. Another detention officer and I loaded the boy into the transport van and headed to the hospital. With the knowledge that the boy had potentially consumed a dangerous amount of medication, I insisted that he stay awake as I rushed to the hospital. With one eye on the road and one eye on the boy, I constantly repeated his name and asked if he could hear me as we made our way to the hospital. When we arrived at the emergency room, the boy did not say a word as we made our way through the doors, and everyone in the waiting room pretended not to stare as two officers and one handcuffed child made our way to the front desk.

While the other detention officer was in the restroom, I knew I had an opportunity to try to get to know the boy, as he was not mad at me since I had not been the one tasked with the duty of handcuffing him. As he sat on the hospital bed, handcuffed to the bedrail, he stared blankly ahead. "Are you OK?" I finally asked as gently as I could. Without taking his eyes off the wall they had been glued to since we arrived, Jose began to cry. Upon the second detention officer's entrance back into the hospital room, the tearful child disappeared, and the scowl was plastered back onto his face.

Over the next year, I watched Jose visibly harden on the outside. He spent approximately three months in detention during his first period of incarceration at the facility, only to be re-arrested and brought back to the facility less than two days after he was released. Jose had a great sense of humor and was always looking to make people laugh while constantly laughing himself. However, due to the long periods that he was ordered to spend in the detention center, he often became what staff called "too comfortable," joking too much with staff and other residents, seeing how far he could push the limits.

"Do they not know who I am?" was one of Jose's go-to phrases each time he perceived another resident to be challenging him in any capacity. Each time Jose made it to phase 4, the highest privilege level that can be earned by residents at the facility, Jose would experience great, sometimes even too much, pride in being on "the highest phase." However, when Jose would act out too much and lose a phase level, he was quick to demonstrate just how much he was unbothered by losing a phase.

Before Jose was sent to a residential placement after his second stay at the detention center, he decided that he wanted to "go out with a bang." While he was walking to his room the night before his transfer, Jose stopped and flipped over a table in West Wing for no apparent reason. As Jose was short, stocky, not very quick, and not at all malicious, staff were able to immediately restrain his legs and arms. Prepared to tackle Jose to the ground, staff informed him as they held him in a restraint, "If you just walk to your room, we don't have to carry you there."

"OK, I'll go," Jose defeatedly responded as he walked to his cell. After several stays in the detention center and a suicide attempt at a residential placement, Jose was ordered to spend a minimum of nine months in the DOC, otherwise known as "prison for kids."

After Jose was ordered to be sent to DOC, he became fixated on what could potentially happen to him in the following weeks. One night, while I went to perform a guard tour and check on all the residents who were in bed, Jose hopped out of bed and was waiting at his door, peering out the window as I passed by his door.

"What's up, Jose?" I asked, observing the sadness on his face. Getting no response, I asked him if he was alright. Jose turned and slowly went to sit on his bed. "Are you worried about going to DOC?" I asked him.

Jose nodded yes and then stood up again. "I just don't understand," he stated, his voice growing louder. "I'm here again because I tried to kill myself in placement, so now they're going to punish me instead of getting me the help that they keep saying I need? You know, because of what I did before I came here the first time, nobody likes me or thinks of me the same. Even my family looks at me different. They say they don't, but I can tell. I'm never going to be able to get my life back."

Hyperaware of any conversation involving suicidal ideation within the detention center, where the rates of attempted suicide are high across the nation, I asked Jose if he was contemplating suicide now. Jose shrugged. "Do you think you can keep from hurting yourself here, Jose?" I questioned. Again, Jose shrugged. Recognizing the signs of suicidality, I asked the control room staff to open Jose's cell door. "Jose, I want to make sure you are safe," I stated calmly. "Can you come with me and sleep in the observation room tonight?"

"See, this is why I never talk to staff, because then you just throw me in OB!" Jose exclaimed as he covered himself with his blanket and lay in bed, refusing to look at me.

I watched Jose lay there for a minute as I contemplated the best method for getting him to an observation room. "Jose, you remember Nathan, who was here a few months ago and went to DOC?"

"No," he muttered.

"East Wing Nathan with the long hair," I described.

"Oh, the ugly-lookin' one?" he asked. "I hated him," Jose declared.

"You know, Nathan was really scared to go to DOC, too," I told Jose. I knew that Jose had a spiritual background. "Every day when I wake up, I say a prayer that Nathan is doing alright there. And I'll do the same thing for you when you go."

Jose considered my statement for a moment before he uncovered himself from under his blanket and looked up at me. He stood up out of bed and remarked, "Alright, we can go to OB," he stated as he walked out of his cell.

In order to evaluate the mentoring and reentry program that I facilitated within the juvenile detention center at that time, I implemented pre- and post-surveys to evaluate residents' responses to the REACH program. The post-test asks several short-answer questions, including "Do you feel that your self-esteem has increased as a result of the REACH program?" "Do you feel that your decision-making skills have increased as a result of the REACH program?" "Do you feel that your understanding of your own goals has increased as a result of the REACH program?" and "Do you feel that your sense of support in working to achieve your goals has increased as a result of the REACH program?" To each question on the survey, which he completed just days before his transport to DOC, Jose wrote, "No, because I am going to DOC to die."

The day before Jose was transported to DOC, I pulled him out of class to speak with him. "How are you feeling about tomorrow?" I questioned him.

Jose shrugged, appearing to attempt to hide all emotion as his eyes glistened slightly, threatening to give him away. "I'm not going to be a bitch in there," Jose stated miserably.

After talking through the potential outcomes of his time at DOC, I reminded Jose of all the people who would be ready to welcome him back home after DOC.

"I'll try to be strong and keep to myself, but I ain't no bitch," Jose adamantly stated as I walked with him out of the visiting room.

"Call me when you get out, alright? I'll be waiting to hear from you," I instructed him.

Much to my surprise, nearly a year and a half later, my phone rang one afternoon while I was at work. "Hi, who is this?" I asked.

"It's Jose. You told me to call you when I got out of DOC," the voice on the other end replied. "Jose? Wow, it's great to hear from you! How are you doing?" I asked him.

"I'm alright. I just got out yesterday," he stated.

"Are you staying with your family?" I asked next.

"Yeah, I'm staying with my mom, and I applied to work at Walmart," he informed me. As I was being called away to speak with a resident at my job simultaneously, I asked Jose if he would have time to call me at 10:00 a.m. the next day.

"Yeah, that'll work," he responded.

When I did not hear from him the next day, I tried calling the number from which he had called me the following day. No one answered, so I left a voicemail asking Jose to give me a callback. As I did not receive a callback, I often wondered what happened to Jose until one day, I saw a new file with Jose's name on it float across my desk while working in the local prosecutor's office. I was reminded once again of how difficult it is to make it out of the justice system once becoming initially involved.

# CHAPTER 4

# ERIC

Eric was a soft-spoken sixteen-year-old boy who typically caused no issues unless he felt that he needed to defend himself and his pride against other residents. Arrested and placed on probation and home detention for small, non-violent offenses and probation violations, Eric was typically well-behaved, especially within a strictly controlled environment, such as the juvenile detention center. Hesitant to talk to people, many of the facility staff did not know Eric well, and many of the other youth found him to be an easy target for their jokes.

When Eric was brought into the juvenile detention center, he did not talk to many of the other residents. Sitting straight-faced for the entirety of most days throughout his stay in detention, Eric often avoided interacting with staff or other residents. One evening after dinner, Eric asked me if he could talk with me in private. We went to the classroom and sat down, and Eric's lip immediately started to tremble.

"What's wrong, Eric?" I asked.

"I don't know how to make things better when I go home," he began to cry. "My mom is always mad at me when I'm there."

"What does she get mad about?" I questioned him.

"She gets mad when I don't come home at night, even though I tell her where I am," he explained, wiping away tears.

"Why do you stay out all night?" I asked.

"Because I go home like she says, and then she just ignores me. I don't feel like my family loves me," Eric cried. "I go home, and my mom just kinda ignores me. And she's always telling me not to discipline my siblings, but I'm used to doing that because I used to take care of them," Eric continued to cry.

Eric and I discussed what he would like to happen when he goes home, as well as his personal goals. As we discussed Eric's feelings and potential ways to improve interactions between him and his family, his tears began to slow down. Finally, he wiped his eyes and appeared to feel better as he headed to bed.

In the following weeks leading up to Eric's release from juvenile detention, I asked him how he was doing each day. Typically, Eric just shrugged in response, giving me a sorrowful look as if he were attempting to convey his feelings to me without allowing the other residents to see.

Although Eric did not return to the facility during the remainder of the time I was employed there and I did not encounter him out in the community, I often think about how well he phrased the feelings of aloneness that many justice-involved juveniles experience throughout their lives. All too often, they act out in response to not feeling loved, accepted, or wanted within their own homes.

# CHAPTER 5

# DERRICK

When I met Derrick, he was a senior in high school and was currently living at a transitional living facility for young adults experiencing homelessness in the city. With long hair that he often tied up into a "man bun," ears pierced, and tank tops that he wore daily, Derrick got along with anyone and everyone and was beloved by most of the girls who passed through the facility. It wasn't until you gained his trust that he would tell you about being adopted and subsequently abused and then eventually disowned by his adoptive family after spending time in a residential youth facility for youth with maladaptive behaviors.

As the school year dragged on, Derrick began to struggle more and more to find the motivation to continue going. As he was making money in his welding training program, he often expressed the feeling that school was a waste of time, no matter how many times I, and others, reminded him that he would have a hard time getting pay increases or other jobs in the future without a high school diploma. In the evenings, I often made it a point to check in with Derrick regarding his homework. We found a routine of microwaving three-minute pizzas at night when he got home from school and work and then managing to at least talk through some of his homework assignments for the night.

Somewhat of an old soul and having had to grow up early, Derrick usually concealed the hurt child within that typically only made an appearance when he talked about his past. However, one night, I had the opportunity to introduce Derrick to a new male mentor—a cool, smooth-talking, laid-back guy. As we were talking, Derrick misheard a word that the mentor, Darnell, said.

"Sorry, what did you say?" Derrick asked.

Darnell repeated himself and said he appreciated that Derrick had asked a question when he didn't understand something. Derrick grinned ear to ear at the praise. Darnell had a tendency to use big words in his everyday speech, by which Derrick was amazed. "My kids were just exuberant when we went to the park yesterday," Darnell stated casually.

Fueled by the joy of receiving acknowledgment from Darnell over his last question, Derrick chimed in. "What does *exuberant* mean?" he asked earnestly. As Darnell explained, Derrick eagerly jotted the word and its definition down in a notebook he happened to have sitting on the table. Not five minutes later, the conversation had turned to Derrick. "Yeah, I was just exuberant at work yesterday!" he announced proudly. I smiled at his eagerness to please the new male in his life yet felt saddened by the thought that he felt so compelled to stand out and receive affirmation from a man he had met not an hour prior.

One evening, I happened to already be at the facility where Derrick was living when he got home from work. "Uh-oh, what's wrong?" I asked when Derrick stormed into the house with his fists balled up and a scowl on his face. Rather than responding, Derrick pushed past me and angrily stomped through the facility and out the backdoor, where I could hear the clanging of metal trashcans as he knocked them over. Knowing that there is often a fine line between wanting to be asked what's wrong and wanting to be left alone, I gave Derrick his space until, eventually, he came and found me in my office and plopped down in a chair.

"Sorry about earlier," he announced with his head down.

"Do you want to talk about it?" I asked gently.

Derrick shrugged, paused, and then launched into his story. "My brother—well, he's not like my blood brother, but he's my brother—did something dumb and got himself fired. And now he left the state with some chick and won't even answer my calls," he said, clearly growing more and more upset as he talked.

After practicing my active listening skills and fully fleshing out the story with him, I finally reminded Derrick that the only person we can control is ourselves. Seemingly satisfied after pondering that piece of advice for a while, Derrick thanked me for listening and wandered off.

By the time I began working with Derrick, he had been approved for an affordable housing voucher through a program offered to youth who had aged out of the foster care system. Although Derrick was incredibly smart, he often worked two jobs and found it difficult to manage his time in between work to figure out how to complete paperwork and other tasks that he did not enjoy. Naturally, this led to a mad panic the day before his voucher expired, and he had yet to find a suitable apartment that would accept his voucher. Reluctant to "save" the youth from situations that they created but also not willing to let his voucher expire in order to teach him a lesson, I helped him hurriedly complete the extension request form and rushed it downtown to the Housing Authority Office while Derrick went to work.

"Thanks for doing that, Sam," Derrick stated gratefully when he got off work that night, and we sat down for our evening microwavable pizza.

After another month of searching for an apartment, Derrick finally settled on a studio apartment priced at $675 per month, of which he would only have to pay a couple hundred. Derrick's move-in date came quickly, and his fear of moving out on his own was tangible as we packed his belongings into the van.

"What am I gonna do without you?" Derrick asked quietly, as we drove to his new apartment with everything he owned in the backseat.

"I'll still be here just the same as I was before you moved out on your own," I reminded him. On the way, we had to stop to purchase an air pump for the air mattress he had purchased for his new place.

Once we picked up his keys from the leasing office, we drove the last couple of blocks to the apartment building. Derrick seemed to shrink farther and farther into the seat as we pulled into the parking lot. However, once we parked, he bravely hopped out and set off to find his new unit. We carried his belongings inside, and then I encouraged him to pay attention as I checked all the faucets and light switches to make sure everything was working. We reviewed his lease so he would know who to contact in what types of situations, and he determined that he was set and would be alright.

"Want a picture in your very first place?" I asked. Derrick

shrugged as he tried not to appear miserable. "You might want one later," I assured him. I snapped the picture while he smiled with his hands in his pockets, standing in the middle of his studio. I hugged Derrick as we both blinked back tears, and he promised to call with any questions or worries.

*Derrick moving into his first apartment.*

I continued checking in with Derrick every few weeks, although it was harder to maintain contact since he was no longer living in a facility. When he texted me to ask how things were going the following June, I asked if he had officially graduated, as he talked about dropping out of school for the entire duration of the second semester of his senior year.

"Yes maam," he texted back.

"So proud of you, congratulations!!" I replied excitedly.

Several months later, Derrick had quit his welding job after "not getting along with the other guys" and was working on and off landscaping gigs while searching for other work.

Derrick texted me asking for assistance filling out his housing voucher renewal form a while later, and I asked him to send me pictures of the forms so I could walk him through the paperwork. The day passed, and I still did not receive the pictures of the documents. Recognizing the importance of helping him complete and submit his voucher renewal on time, I followed up with Derrick regarding the photos the following day.

"My bad, Sam, I know I need to prioritize this. I'll send them when I get home from work," he promised.

The following morning, I woke up to the fifteen images of the form, mostly already completed. I called Derrick, and we talked through the remainder of the document that needed to be filled out. After catching up for a minute, Derrick thanked me and hung up to leave for work. He assured me he knew where to deliver the forms, and I reminded him of the importance of doing so on time.

A few days passed, and Derrick did not confirm whether he had delivered his form to the housing office. Concerned that he would lose his voucher, I called one of my former colleagues who still lived near Derrick, and I knew they had a positive relationship and talked frequently. I explained my concerns to him and asked him if he would check up on him.

My friend called back a couple of hours later and said, "It sounds bad, but he's OK."

I was instantly filled with dread. He informed me that Derrick had overdosed on some type of pills and was in the hospital on a psychiatric hold, as they were concerned that he took too much of the medication intentionally. Visions of Derrick walking around in his white tank top, constantly smiling and charming everyone around him, swirled through my head. My former colleague explained that he had spoken with Derrick over the phone while he was in the hospital and that Derrick told him that another young girl, with whom all three of us were familiar, had come over to his house and offered him some unknown pills. Hesitant to take them but not wanting to be a buzzkill, Derrick popped some of his own pills that he had at his apartment, hopped on a bus to go to work a few hours later, and started feeling sick and ended up in the hospital. I thanked my friend for always being there for Derrick and asked him to keep me posted.

A few days later, Derrick texted me, apologizing for not

responding to my texts and explaining that it had been a "long week." He assured me that he was alright, and I continue to hear from him every now and again.

Derrick seems to have achieved the goal of living independently and maintaining some form of employment—accomplishments that many young men who have experienced such difficult childhoods are unable to do. While he still struggles with having no family (blood-related or adoptive) to call, he has defied the odds that were stacked against him since day one.

# CHAPTER 6

## ORLANDO

Even before I created the juvenile reentry program or started my nonprofit organization, I worked closely with Orlando for nearly seven years. Hardly weighing one hundred pounds and never seeming too concerned with his appearance, Orlando was one of the most laid-back kids with whom I had ever engaged. Typically content just going with the flow of life, he insisted that his only goal was to become a successful "farmer." I was constantly reminding Orlando of the fact that growing marijuana is not yet legal in Indiana.

Although for the past eight years I had celebrated holidays and Orlando and his siblings' birthdays with several of them together, a couple of years ago, Orlando moved into an apartment with his girlfriend and began having even less frequent contact with his family. I picked Orlando up at his apartment to celebrate his birthday, and he came trotting across the parking lot and embraced me.

"What have you been up to lately?" I asked him.

"Oh, you know, same old same old," he replied, shaking his head.

"Have you thought any more about getting a legal job?" I asked him. "Because when I see you selling and 'going mobile' on social media every night, I really worry about you," I remarked.

"I don't really know anything else that I have any interest in," Orlando responded.

"Have you been working on getting your driver's license?" I asked, sensing that it may be time to change the subject.

"I tried to take it and failed!" he responded. "Fuck that test and fuck anybody that tries to make me take it!" Orlando exploded.

I realized it was time for another subject change. "Want to stop and get some pizza?" I asked.

After ordering a medium pepperoni and two pina colada juices, I tested the waters. "So if I helped you study and took you to the BMV to retake your driver's test, would you be up for that?" I questioned cautiously.

"Yeah, I'd be alright with that," Orlando replied, seeming to forget his previous outburst.

After lunch, I drove Orlando back to his apartment and instructed him to open his belated Christmas present. As he unwrapped the outfits I had sorted out for him from some clothing donations at my organization, Orlando appeared relieved. "Thank you, Sam. All my clothes have kinda just disappeared. This helps a lot."

The following Saturday morning, I texted Orlando that I was picking him up around 10:30 a.m. for a mentoring group session. Orlando responded that his friend, Danny, had just been released from juvenile detention and he could not come to mentoring because they needed to hang out. I encouraged Orlando to invite Danny too.

"He's not really into that kinda thing," Orlando texted back.

"Tell him Sam says he needs to come," I replied.

"Wow, alright, I guess we'll be there," he responded a couple of minutes later. After convincing both boys to attend the mentoring group and establishing that Danny would pick up Orlando and they would both meet me at the group, I said a quick prayer that they would actually make it to the church for the group. As I was driving to the session, Orlando texted me. "I got somebody coming to pick something up so we might be a lil late," he stated.

"Remember when I said I wanted to come pick you up so this wouldn't happen?" I replied.

"Remember when I told you I might be busy this morning? Sometimes I do be busy," Orlando texted back. Knowing myself well enough to know that I would regret my response if I did not cool off before replying, I did not respond.

Twenty minutes and a lot of deep breaths later, I texted, "I'm at the group, so come on in if you make it. You and Danny can decide what your priorities are."

Nearly half an hour into the session, Orlando and Danny made their appearance. "Sorry, my mom was supposed to come buy some bud, but she was taking forever," Orlando explained casually.

While I was driving another of my boys to an interview a couple of weeks after, he mentioned that Orlando had recently been released from jail. As I usually kept close tabs on Orlando and his siblings, I nearly choked on my gum as I asked what he meant.

"Yeah, he got locked up and just got out," he responded.

I immediately messaged Orlando. "Were you locked up recently?" I questioned, unaware that he had been arrested since his previous stint in a local juvenile detention center over the past summer.

"How'd you hear about that?" Orlando responded.

"I work with a lot of kids that know you," I replied. "What happened?"

"It's a long story. You'll never believe what for," Orlando texted.

"Possession or dealing?" I asked, thinking about all the times I had cautioned him against both.

"No, you literally won't believe it," he responded.

"OK, then what?" I asked.

"Battery," he replied.

My heart sank as I thought about my easy-going kid who was always sensitive and aware of others' needs. "Against someone in your family?" I asked, aware of the volatile relationship that he had with his family members.

"I'd rather talk about it in person," he replied.

The following week, I finally made it to Orlando's apartment to discuss his recent arrest. As usual, Orlando walked briskly to my car, arms open wide to embrace me. "Hey Sam," he stated, sounding like he was dreading the conversation he knew was about to follow.

"Do you want to sit outside?" I asked him.

"Sure," he replied.

"So what happened?" I asked.

Orlando stood, shifting from foot to foot, nervously twisting his hands around in his sweatshirt pockets. "It was so crazy," he stated, seeming hesitant to launch into the story.

Suddenly, his neighbor exited her apartment, quickly and loudly telling Orlando that she'd been sick but would have the clothes washed and returned soon. "Oh, hi," she stated in my direction, appearing to see me in front of her for the first time. "Sorry to interrupt," she exclaimed as she continued talking to Orlando.

As his neighbor began slowly walking out into the parking lot, I suggested that maybe it would be easier to talk inside. Orlando agreed and pushed the front door open, where his girlfriend was sweeping the hardwood living room floor.

"Alright, now what happened?" I reminded Orlando to continue with the story.

"Well, to make a long story short, I bought some Wendy's for her," he stated, nodding toward his girlfriend. "And her sister ate the frosty, so I started talking shit to her, you know, because I had bought that food for Alecia."

I nodded.

"And I wasn't going to put my hands on her, but then she hit me, and she grabbed something from the counter. I didn't even know what it was until Alecia yelled that it was a knife. So I hit her. And then I hit her a few more times, but it was all in self-defense. She weighs like three times what I weigh—like two hundred and forty pounds!" he exclaimed.

"And then what happened?" I asked.

"So her sister ran outside screaming, and I panicked and packed up my stuff and ran next door to hide," he stated. "Then I thought the coast was clear, so I walked outside, and then fuckin' twelve showed up. At first, they didn't know it was me they were looking for, but then they asked me a couple of questions and threw the cuffs on," he stated. "So they took me to intake, and I was pissed 'cause I went in with like $1,285, and then they set my bond at $1,300 and wouldn't accept anything less. Then the next day, Alecia and a few of her friends showed up with the bond money and got me out," he concluded.

Seeming oblivious to any other ramifications of the case other than the fact that his cash still had not been returned to him from the jail, I asked Orlando when his court hearing was scheduled.

"I don't know yet. They literally didn't tell me anything at the jail. They just told me I would get something in the mail," he explained.

"So you know it's really risky for you to be getting high and especially to be dealing, particularly when you may be on pre-trial, right?" I asked him.

"Yeah, Sam, I know," he stated, sounding defeated.

"I can help you get a legal job. Just remember that," I stated before I left the apartment.

Later in the evening, Orlando messaged me. "Hey Sam, I think I'd like to take you up on that offer to help me find a job," he stated. Delighted, I told him we would meet up soon to create his résumé so he could begin applying for jobs. "Thank u so much Sam," he messaged back.

A few days later, I sent Orlando a message that I would be in the area that evening if he was free for me to drop by and help him create a résumé. "I'm out at the school with my girl," he texted back. "Alright it's up to both of you then," I replied. "I can come to the school and help you with it, or we can wait until another day." As I somewhat expected, I did not receive a response. This was typical, as many of the young men I worked with had a tendency to become involved with girls who sometimes would decide to kick them out of their often-shared apartments or parents' homes if they suspected they were talking to another woman, regardless of whether that woman was their social worker. The next time I heard from Orlando was when I wished him "happy birthday" over Facebook Messenger later that summer.

"Thank you Sam," followed by a black heart emoji was his response.

Several months later, I received a message from Orlando asking if I could help him look for a job. Excitedly, I connected him with one of my interns and informed him that she would help him search for employment. While briefly checking my social media one afternoon, I came across an advertisement for a landscaping company that was urgently hiring. I texted a screenshot of the advertisement to my intern, and she shared it with Orlando. Less than three days later, Orlando informed her that he was starting his new job with the company. However, just a few weeks later, the intern informed me that Orlando was back on the hunt for a job.

# CHAPTER 7

# JASON

Although I worked with Jason when he was a young child, due to knowing his family from the community, I lost much contact with him while he was incarcerated from age fourteen to eighteen. Each time he neared release, he got into a fight or demonstrated some violent behavior which led to continuously extended stays within the facility. However, once Jason was released at age eighteen, I began working with him again as he desired.

Once Jason was finally released, he returned home to his family, who resided about twenty minutes from me. Though I did not meet to catch up with Jason for a couple of months after his release, I was able to somewhat stay in touch via social media. He landed a job working nights shortly after he returned home. When I stopped by to drop Jason's younger brother off at their house one afternoon, his mom informed me that Jason had been arrested the previous day for having some pills in his pocket when he was pulled over for a traffic stop. As she explained the situation to me, my mind repeatedly circled back to the fact that Jason did not yet even possess a driver's license.

A couple of weeks later, I arranged a time to meet up with Jason. I showed up where he was staying with a couple of pizzas for him and his brothers and their roommate. When I walked into the house, all three brothers greeted me with hugs. I then noticed the two people on the couch who made no movement or indication that they noticed a new person standing in the house. I was unsure of whether they were asleep or too high to notice that they had company. I then noted the empty kitchen cabinets and half-eaten bowl of ramen noodles in the fridge; the home was nearly uninhabitable.

"How have you all been?" I asked the boys.

Jason grinned and said he was doing "'ight" but had just gotten out of jail again.

"What happened?" I asked, refraining from telling him that I was already aware of the last time he had been arrested that same month.

"I got pulled over with some weed," he nonchalantly said as he began pulling paraphernalia out of his pockets and placing it all on the kitchen table.

"Your little brother doesn't need to be seeing all this, Jason," I told him.

"Are you two looking for jobs or what?" I asked the older two boys.

"Well, see, I was working a real good construction job, but then my sister's boyfriend got pissed at her and wouldn't take me to work one day. Then they fired me," Jason explained.

I looked to the next brother for his explanation behind his unemployment.

"Well, a lot of times I stay with my girlfriend's family, and they stay like thirty minutes from here, so then I'm kinda out of luck," he explained.

"Sam, my mom needs me to help her go load up a mattress. Can you take me back there real quick?" Jason asked as he shoved his pockets full of marijuana, wax, and other paraphernalia.

"Jason, I want to drive you, but I can't take you in my car with all that in your pockets," I told him.

"What? Are you serious?" Jason asked me in disbelief.

"Yes! That all is illegal here, you know that," I stated.

"See, you should've just let me put it in *my* pockets!" Jason's twelve-year-old brother yelled.

I looked at Jason sternly. "This is a problem. You better not be having your little brother transport drugs for you," I stated firmly.

Jason continued to stare at me in disbelief.

"I'll drive you if you leave all that stuff here," I told him.

Jason looked over at his brother.

"Hey, you already bought it. I ain't giving you no money back." His brother laughed.

Jason shook his head in disbelief as he called his mom for a ride.

"I'm sorry," I told Jason. "You know I would give you a ride if you didn't have that on you. I can't risk or condone it," I explained.

"I know, Sam. I can't even be mad. Some people just don't like that, I get it," he replied.

In an attempt to provide Jason with a positive male role model who could devote more time to helping him search for a job, I paired him up with a volunteer mentor through my nonprofit. Jason and his mentor seemed to hit it off, and Jason was working at a restaurant just a few weeks later. However, as his new mentor and I continued with our weekly check-in sessions, where we debriefed and discussed how everything was going with providing mentorship to Jason, his mentor noted that Jason had told him he was mad that the restaurant would not allow him to take the Fourth of July off work. The week following the holiday, Jason's mentor informed me that he was no longer working at the restaurant but that they were looking into new job opportunities.

In order to make attaining and maintaining a decent job more feasible, Jason and his mentor determined that their next goal would be to obtain Jason's driver's license. Due to having numerous points against his license without ever having received a license, both were unsure of whether he would be granted a license even if he could pass the test. A couple of months passed, and I reached out to Jason to inquire about whether he needed me to take him to the BMV for his driver's test. Because nobody in his family had a registered, plated, and insured car, it would be necessary for Jason to find someone else who would allow him to borrow their car to take the driving test. "I actually got my license!" Jason replied when I asked him if he wanted me to take him to the BMV. "And I bought my own car," he stated next.

However, less than three weeks later, I again checked in with Jason regarding his job search. "Well, honestly, I don't want to work a job if the money isn't worth my time. I need to make more than what I'm making now," he explained, referencing his illegal marijuana distribution.

"Understandable," I replied. However, I assured him we could find him a local restaurant where he could work and make great tips. "Do you still have your license and car?" I asked.

"My car doesn't work," Jason responded. As I found myself

feeling incredibly defeated by the constant struggle to help Jason and many others make progress and achieve their goals, I tried to imagine how defeated he and many others like him must be feeling as they continuously take one step forward and three steps back.

Several months later, I had the opportunity to co-host the founder of Homeboy Industries, the largest gang rehabilitation and reentry program in the world, at the local university where I teach as an adjunct professor. Several of us at the university coordinated a panel discussion with formerly incarcerated individuals, providing a platform to elevate their voices and share their experiences within the justice system. I asked Jason if he would like to speak on the panel.

"Sure that sounds cool," he texted back before asking whether there would be food and how many people would be in the audience. Knowing that he does not have a valid driver's license, I confirmed with Jason multiple times that he would not be driving himself to the event. He assured me that his girlfriend would be driving him there. On the day of the panel, I was somewhat lacking in my belief that Jason would show up, let alone on time. However, an hour before the event, Jason texted me that he had arrived but didn't know where to park. I walked outside to help him navigate to the correct parking lot and was less than pleased to see Jason pulling into the parking lot, alone in the car. I chose to pick my battle that day and simply told Jason I was glad he made it safely.

Jason did a fantastic job speaking on the panel. When asked what we as the community can do to better support individuals as they reintegrate into the community post-incarceration, Jason responded with an explanation of the importance of simply having people available to assist with what might seem like simple tasks. "I don't know who these people are or how she does it, but whenever I ask Sam for help looking for school or for work opportunities, she just sends people to help me," he stated, grinning. "It makes a big difference."

*Jason speaking on the reentry panel at Valparaiso University.*

While it sometimes feels like there are countless setbacks as I continue to work with such a vulnerable population, Jason reminded me that day that sometimes the most important thing we can do for each other is simply to show up.

# CHAPTER 8

## DANNY

Having spent a majority of the past three years in juvenile detention, many staff members anticipated that Danny would age out of the juvenile system at eighteen and either overdose or be killed in a drug deal. Danny was hardly 5'5" and came from affluent suburbia, yet he walked with a swagger that was intended to indicate that he was from "the hood." Typically very respectful, Danny rarely caused issues in the detention center but dealt and used drugs heavily during the short periods when he was not incarcerated. After several long periods of incarceration in the juvenile detention center, Danny was released shortly before his eighteenth birthday. Three days later, he was brought in for possession of paraphernalia, high as a kite. Danny spent his eighteenth birthday in the detention center, with staff constantly discussing with him the importance of changing his ways, and while Danny seemed receptive, he also did not seem to believe that changing was truly an option for him.

When I arrived at the detention center for my shift one winter afternoon, I was immediately aware that there was an incident in progress. One of the residents was refusing to leave the classroom to go to his room, and two other residents, including Danny, were refusing to leave the room in solidarity with their friend. When staff finally cleared out the room of all residents aside from the boy who was refusing to stand up, the other residents were ordered to go to another room. Danny slowly sauntered around, subtly defying staff's orders to clear out the multipurpose room.

"Go to your room, Danny!" the supervisor finally yelled.

Danny, shifting from one foot to another, was near tears as he stammered about all the reasons why he had not been trying to ignore staff's instructions. After ten minutes of pleading his case, the supervisor decided to give Danny a break and instructed him to return to the classroom, where Danny proceeded to sit down and sulk in silence for the next hour.

"How are your classes coming, Danny?" I asked one afternoon during my shift at the detention center.

"Oh, I graduated today," Danny replied nonchalantly.

"You graduated high school today? Congratulations! That is a big deal!" I exclaimed.

Danny shrugged yet glanced up with a small grin on his face as he took in my excitement over his graduation.

"So now what?" I asked him.

"I guess I just have to wait on the school to send me my diploma, and then I just wait to get out of this place," he explained.

"Do you think you'll get your time cut since you finally graduated?" I asked.

"I think I got too many phase losses in the past few weeks to get out early," Danny stated as he stared at the floor.

However, several days later, much to everyone's surprise, Danny was released from detention as a result of obtaining his high school diploma before his anticipated release date.

The following Saturday morning, I met up with Danny and another of my eighteen-year-old boys at a Saturday mentoring group nearby. When the three of us arrived at the mentoring group, we walked into the basement of the church where the session was being held. Danny, having been released from juvenile detention just two days prior, was still walking with swag and hanging his pants down around his hips. All eyes were on Danny and his friend, Orlando, as we walked through the group of other youth involved in the mentoring program. Throughout the session, every time a comment was made in the general direction of Danny, he loudly responded, "Hell yeah!" However, after the first hour of the group, the "hell yeahs" began to fade out as Danny seemed to remember that there were other possible responses to use.

When a wheelchair-bound potential investor in the mentoring group made an appearance at the church, I encouraged Orlando and Danny to help carry his wheelchair downstairs to the mentoring room. Very carefully, the boys both carried a side of the wheelchair holding the man down the stairs. After helping transport him down the stairs and feeling a sense of helpfulness, both Orlando and Danny seemed to carry themselves slightly different, appearing to feel a sense of pride and usefulness over being able to help someone else.

I picked Danny up for the Saturday mentoring group the following weekend, and we went to pick up another program participant, Hector. On the way to the home where Hector was staying at the time, Danny told me about the jobs he had applied for and asked numerous questions about how to lease an apartment.

"I have the money, but apartments keep asking me for pay stubs to show how I make the money," Danny complained. "So I guess I've gotta get a legit job."

I advised him on several stores to apply at, including Menards. Once we arrived at the home where Hector was staying, Danny hopped out of the car to allow Hector into the back seat of my two-door car. Hector sat down in the car, and I turned around in shock.

"You really think you're going to go to mentoring smelling this strong like marijuana?" I asked him incredulously.

"What are you talking about?" Hector asked, his eyes wide, trying to hold back a grin. Danny sat in the front seat, eyes equally wide as he attempted to hold back a smile and shook his head toward Hector.

"Hector, do you have anything on you, or do you just smell like a walking blunt?" I asked him.

"Nah, I just smell like that," Hector responded.

"Danny, do you have anything on you?" I asked.

"No way, I've got too much respect for you to do that, Sam," he adamantly stated as he laughed at Hector.

Two weeks later, I picked Danny up for our weekly mentoring session. Because we had spare time before the group began, we went to walk around a local college campus, as Danny had been talking on and off about college as an option now that he had graduated high school. As we walked through the library, Danny plopped down at the blood pressure machine. "I haven't taken my blood pressure in years," Danny stated as the machine clamped down on his arm. As we continued walking around the library, we discovered the snack shop, which was closed. "Think anybody would notice if I snatched one of these?" he asked, pointing to a bag of hot Cheetos.

"Yes, definitely," I responded.

As we walked to the car, Danny appeared deep in thought. "You know, I really have no idea what I want to do now that I'm done with high school," Danny mused.

The following day, I texted Danny to see when he wanted to go to Menards to submit an application. He did not respond.

The following Saturday, I took Danny and another one of the boys involved in my organization's programming to see the two properties that had been donated to my nonprofit organization in an attempt to get them motivated about the organization and the opportunities that the business would provide for them and for other youth and young adults in similar situations. We walked through the houses, and I explained what I envisioned each room being used for. "Damn, Sam. This is gonna take a lot of work," the boys mused as we walked through the properties.

Later that evening, Danny texted me, "Hey I've got some friends who said they are interested in helping with fixing up the houses."

Several months later, having been told by another of my boys that Danny might have been kicked out of his parents' home, I texted him to check in.

"Yeah I been doin okay. Lookin for a new crib rn. And still tryna get a job i put in a lot of apps for diff places jus waitin to hear sum," Danny responded.

Several different juveniles involved in the REACH program had been informing me that Danny had been using a lot of hard drugs lately. I had not heard from him in several weeks, so I was concerned that Danny might be spiraling. I sent him a message that I had heard the local Menards was doing on-the-spot interviews.

"Wow thanks I had no idea they were doin that appreciate the information and its good hearing from u again," Danny replied.

Several months passed before I heard from Danny again. When I did, it was about 10:00 p.m. on a weeknight. "Hey," the first text read. *Oh good, maybe he is ready to work with the program and get a job now*, I thought excitedly to myself. Before I could respond, he texted again, "If you still work at juvenile can you tell Lacy that I love her and she needs to listen to her mom so she can come home to us." I rolled my eyes and couldn't help but feel slightly deflated as I thought about the vicious cycle that often leads justice-involved people to each other and makes it incredibly difficult for people to change their ways of thinking and living.

A few more months passed, and I began working in the local prosecutor's office. One day, I saw a search warrant float across my desk with Danny's name on it. Several days later, two new files filled with high-level felony charges against him were created. The charges and files continued to build against Danny over time. Though I occasionally texted him to check in over the following months, I rarely received a response.

However, out of the blue one February evening, Danny texted, "Is this still Sam number." After assuring him that it was still my number, Danny replied, "Have any advice for me I'm down kinda bad rn and need to find a job or something to get me away from all it."

We arranged to meet in the next couple of days to discuss his situation and employment goals. After a two-day snowstorm concluded, I picked Danny up at his parents' house to take him to chat over breakfast. "Outside," I texted him when I pulled up to the house. Danny came jumping through the snow like a jackrabbit from the backside of the house, dusting his shoes off with a broom that was propped against the garage before running to my car. He glanced around before hopping into my car, giving me the sense that he was in deeper trouble than I had originally suspected. As soon as Danny slid into the passenger seat, he confirmed this to be true.

"I owe a lot of people money," Danny blurted at one point as he hastily caught me up on the past two years of his life, explaining why he desperately needed to find a job before he wound up dead. Before I even pulled the car out of the driveway, the severity of Danny's drug use was blatantly obvious. He could not quit swaying his head back and forth as he talked and never stopped moving. Having not seen Danny in quite a while, it was unclear to me whether his drug use over time had damaged his body or whether he was high at the time. Although Danny promised me he had not "smoked weed since last night," I had a difficult time believing that he was sober.

We walked into a cafe downtown to find some breakfast and talk. I pointed out the QR code on the wall that had to be scanned to access the cafe's menu. "This is a pretty expensive place," Danny said partially to himself.

"Breakfast is on me," I assured him.

"Really?" Danny asked, sounding shocked. "Can I get some biscuits and gravy?" Danny asked me.

"You can get whatever you want," I reiterated.

"If I buy a coffee, can you buy the breakfast?" he asked quietly.

"I'll buy them both, Danny," I explained again.

"Wow, thank you so much, Sam," he said.

"What's going on with your arms?" I asked Danny as we sat down, and he continuously scratched at his arms and legs.

"Oh, I have Psoriasis," he stated as he continued scratching. "I couldn't afford my meds anymore. They're like $4 a pill, and I'm supposed to take them twice a day."

As we sat and ate, I texted a friend of mine who was looking for pro bono clients so she could complete her internship and obtain her degree in pastoral counseling. Danny, totally willing to accept any services that wouldn't throw him farther into debt, was thrilled at the opportunity to begin counseling with her the following week. We also managed to start Danny's application to Ivy Tech and connected him with one of my interns to assist with his job search. As I drove Danny back to his parents' house a couple of hours later, he stated, "That was the most I've ever done in a day," sounding satisfied.

The following Sunday, I drove to Danny's parents' house to pick him up for church. After waiting in the car for nearly ten minutes for Danny to emerge from the house, I finally grew impatient enough to call him. "Sorry, I'm just putting a coat on and coming out," Danny said quickly when he answered the phone.

"Alright," I responded, hanging up the phone.

Less than ten seconds later, Danny called back. "Hey, Sam, I've got a friend with me. She's a girl. Is it cool if she comes with us too?"

"Of course, as long as you both hurry up," I responded.

Danny and his friend came sauntering out of the house, his friend grabbing onto him to hold him up as he nearly wiped out on a sheet of ice while walking to my car. They both slid into my car, and I gave Danny a sideways look when I noticed his watery, red eyes. "I only got like two hours of sleep last night," Danny immediately stated. As I pulled out of the driveway to head to church, Danny asked, "So where are we headed, NA?"

It never fails to both humor and humble me when kiddos agree to go somewhere with me, apparently with no recollection of where we are headed.

As Danny vaped almost constantly on the way to church, I warned him to take a big hit so he wouldn't need to use it while in church. We walked in, both Danny and his friend stopping every few steps. I looked back to make sure they were following, and Danny was tying his friend's sweatshirt. When she noticed me staring, she laughed nervously. "Teamwork," she said, chuckling.

"There's breakfast foods and coffee over there if you want any," I told them, pointing out the church's refreshment table in the corner. Danny and his friend rushed over to the table as if they hadn't eaten in days. They each walked back to the table where I had saved them seats with a handful of muffins, pastries, fruit snacks, and coffee in Styrofoam cups stacked three cups tall.

After they spent the first twenty minutes of the service scarfing down their breakfast, Danny appeared to be intently listening to the pastor while his friend stayed glued to her phone. Halfway through the sermon, the pastor began speaking on forgiveness, and I noticed Danny nodding and making a quick sign of the cross. He too soon turned his attention to his phone, the pair sitting next to each other, scratching, scrolling on their phones, and eating fruit snacks. However, when the pastor said, "Let's bow our heads and pray," both immediately put down their phones and bowed their heads for the prayer.

As we were walking out of the church after service, one of my close friends, who had been sitting with us throughout the service, recommended that next time I detox my people before bringing them to church. We both laughed nervously, and I thought about how grateful I am to belong to a church family that doesn't blink an eye when I bring along clients who are battling addiction, experiencing homelessness, living with serious mental illness, or who walk back and forth to the refreshment table twenty-five times during one church service.

A few days later, I texted Danny to ask if he wanted to go to a Celebrate Recovery meeting with me. "Yeah sure cool," he replied and then asked what time he should be ready for me to pick him up. When I pulled up at his parents' house to pick him up that evening, I texted him to let him know I was outside. I received no answer and called him a few minutes later. Still no answer. Five minutes later, I was about to drive away when Danny called me back. "Yo Sam, hey I have a friend here with me. She's a girl. Can she come with us?"

"That's fine but hurry up!" I told him, as the meeting would be starting in less than ten minutes. Danny and his friend came hustling out of the house and hopped in the car.

When we arrived at Celebrate Recovery, we all took a seat in the back row, then Danny quickly walked out of the room. Slightly concerned, as he was very jittery and seemed to be acting stranger than normal, I walked out of the room and toward the bathrooms to make sure he was alright. I heard Danny talking loudly on his phone in the bathroom, so I went back to the main room to join the group. Several minutes later, Danny rejoined us in the room but then left again shortly after. He did not return to the meeting, so we went searching for him throughout the church once the event ended. Nowhere to be found, I called Danny and got no answer. His friend said she was unable to get a hold of him either. I finally texted him and asked whether he had left or if we needed to wait on him. "Im sorry Sam i swear i was coming back i got a ride and he fucked me and now i dont have a ride back there." Shocked and furious, I did not reply but informed his friend that Danny had left and asked her where she needed to be dropped off. As I was driving her home, Danny texted me, testing the water. "Im lowkey stranded," he texted. I shook my head at his nerve to subtly ask for a ride after ditching out on the meeting and did not respond.

The following day, Danny texted me to apologize again and explained that he had to leave the meeting to deal with an urgent situation. He then asked if I knew of any shelters in the area, as his parents had kicked him out of their home. I told him where to go and that he needed to arrive in the morning to be possibly admitted into the shelter program. At 7:00 p.m., Danny texted me that he was pulling up at the shelter. I reminded him that I had told him he needed to go in the morning and that nobody would be there to do an intake that late in the evening. "Ok do you know where I can sleep outside that the police won't get called?" he texted me. "I have an extra sweatshirt so I think I'll be warm enough." Unsure of whether he was truly out of options but also knowing that there were no shelters available in the area to direct him at that point, I directed Danny to go to the shelter in the morning if he was serious about trying to stay there.

I did not hear back from Danny for a few days until he texted me that he had checked himself into rehab in Indianapolis since he didn't have anywhere to stay. A week or two later, Danny texted me that he had moved to Indianapolis and was staying with a friend down there and looking for a job. The next time I heard from him was several weeks later when he texted me that he was staying at the Oxford house, working two jobs, and was sixty days sober. "Very proud of you, keep up the great work," I responded.

Several months later, I was in a virtual visit with another of my boys who was incarcerated in the county jail, when he informed me that Danny had died of an overdose. When I asked him where he had heard that, he told me that "his girl" had seen their friends posting about his death on social media. Immediately after our visit ended, I scoured social media, local obituaries, and the internet for anything indicating that Danny had passed away. Finding nothing, I chalked the situation up to mistaken information but continued to listen and watch for additional information while hoping and praying that he was safe.

Many people who have worked with Danny over the years in both the juvenile and adult justice systems have stated he will either end up dead or in prison, often attributing his behaviors to stubbornness, poor attitude, or both. However, many of those same people never learned that his sister died of an overdose and that the genetics of addiction and the pain of losing a family member to drugs significantly increase one's likelihood of engaging in drug use and other illegal activity. Nearly two years later, I heard from Danny from within prison, serving an eight year sentence.

# CHAPTER 9

## ELIAS

Having spent years in the DOC, juvenile detention centers, and various residential placements, Elias was one of the juveniles who was frequently labeled by detention staff as a "career criminal." He had several tattoos, including one next to his eye, an unpredictable temper, very institutional-like manners, and a history of assaulting staff at the detention center. Many officers groaned when he was admitted yet again to our facility. Elias was a force to be reckoned with. Determined to become a barber, Elias frequently preached about being different and finding God yet constantly battled with himself to escape his old ways and habits.

As do many who find themselves in juvenile detention centers, Elias lacked the privilege of having a positive male role model while growing up. One of the male detention officers, Tony, was a common favorite among the older residents. He was admired for his size, stature, demeanor, and no-nonsense attitude. One Thursday afternoon, three residents received a phase loss (one hour in their room plus a loss of one privilege level in the behavior program), including Elias. The next day, I was watching the older residents as they played basketball in the gym, and Elias was sitting out for the day due to back pain from a gunshot wound he received the previous summer. Sitting in a chair next to me, Elias had been telling me about Santa Muerte and sharing his justification for stealing religious items that "God led him to." Tony sauntered into the gym and began playing basketball with some of the boys and glanced over at Elias.

"What's up, man?" Tony asked him casually.

"Just chillin'," Elias responded as he quickly glanced up at him.

As Tony went back to shooting hoops with the other residents, Elias sat silently for a couple of minutes, then suddenly turned to me. "You think Tony's mad at me for getting in trouble?" Elias questioned me, his voice full of concern.

Holding back a smile, I responded, "What did you get in trouble for?"

"Passing a note," he answered.

"No, I don't think he's mad at you," I assured him.

Elias shook his head yet continued to appear pensive as he contemplated whether or not Tony was mad that he had gotten into trouble for passing a note during class.

Over the following weeks, I witnessed Elias's short fuse and mind-consuming rage on several different occasions. My first glimpse into this side of Elias occurred one night while I was taking the residents one at a time to make phone calls to their parents. I had just left Elias on the phone with his mother and was talking with another resident when Elias came barreling off West Wing, where the younger residents are housed. His face flushed red and his fists clenched, Elias was furiously pacing back and forth as if he were trying to avoid hitting something or someone.

"What happened?" I asked him, alarmed that he might snap.

"The fucking phone cut out again while I was talking to my momma!" he yelled.

"Elias, it's alright. We'll call her back right now," I stated as soothingly as I could manage.

Although Elias calmed down once the phone was reconnected and his mother answered our call, I recognized the short fuse that I had been warned he had but had not yet experienced for myself.

The following week, Elias was walking off East Wing to head to the gym with some of the other older residents. "Is Julie coming to work tonight?" Elias questioned another staff member.

"Yep," the officer replied.

"I hope she gets hit by a car on her way in," Elias stated.

"That's two points," the staff member stated to Elias.

"For what?" Elias cried.

"For saying you hope my coworker gets hit by a car," the staff member retorted back.

"You a bitch!" Elias shouted back at him.

"That's another two," the staff member responded calmly.

Realizing that he was just two more points away from a phase loss, which included an hour in his cell and a loss of a privilege phase, Elias was visibly furious. He threw himself down in a chair, and I walked over to attempt to calm him down before he thought any more about the points he had lost.

"Elias, it's OK. You're fine," I stated.

"It's not fine. I just lost four points!" he shrieked. Recognizing how little control he had over the situation, Elias decided to implement what little control he did have without giving a clear reason for the staff member to give him the last two points for his phase loss. Elias began training his eyes on the staff member, boldly and obviously staring him down. At first, the staff member and I both pretended not to notice, hoping he would soon grow tired of staring. However, as we made our way down the hallway into the gym to play volleyball, Elias continued to stare him down. The staff member finally asked Elias why he continued to stare at him. Elias shouted, "I'm allowed to stare at you, nigga!" Throughout stretches and his five laps around the gym, Elias continued to stare. "My back hurts. I can't play in the game," Elias informed me once he completed his laps, slowly and defiantly.

"Are you sure?" I asked him, though he was already positioning himself to sit next to the staff member who was at the center of his rage. While I felt confident that Elias was about to go off and attack my colleague, he eventually stopped staring and seemed to forget his previous anger when he realized he was not going to receive a response back.

One night, as I was distributing nightly medications to the residents, Elias swallowed his melatonin and then asked if he could speak to me in private once I was finished distributing the residents' medications.

"Sure," I replied. "I'll come get you as soon as I'm finished." Once I had distributed all the meds, I approached Elias, who was sitting alone at a table. "You ready to talk?" I asked.

He nodded and got up to follow me into the classroom.

"What's up?" I asked him as we both sat down facing each other.

Elias stared ahead for a second before stating, "Hold on," as he appeared to both battle tears that were threatening to flow while also trying to choose what to say. With fingers pressed against his eyes in an attempt to hold back the tears, he finally lost any control that he had. Tears began flowing before he could form any words. "I'm always wearing a mask, and I can't ever show people who I really am or they'll think I'm weak. I feel sad and depressed all the time, but I put on a smile and act all happy. I'm ashamed when I think of all the people I hurt in the past, and I actually really like to help people, but that's not what people expect out of me. They expect that I'm just going to go back to my old ways," he managed to get out as he sobbed.

"Are you scared to get out soon?" I asked him.

"Yeah, I'm scared that I'll go back to my old ways because I always want to impress my dad. He was never in my life so when he came back and wanted his son to be just like him, I wanted to impress him. He got me into drugs, the gang, all that shit." Wiping at his tears as they continued to fall, Elias looked at me with eyes full of despair as he continued to tell his story. Elias spoke of his desire to be released, start going to church, get a job, attend Narcotics Anonymous, and stay as busy as possible to avoid temptations to go back to his old ways. Because Elias seemed comforted by the idea of planning for the future so that he could be more prepared to face the real world upon release, I asked him to create a list of positive qualities about himself the following day so that we could begin creating his résumé.

When I was doing the first guard tour of my shift the following day, I asked Elias if he had created his list. He shook his head excitedly and brought the list to me as soon as the residents were released from their rooms after quiet hour. "Punctual, personable, motivated," the list read.

"What's that one mean?" Elias asked me as he pointed to one of his listed qualities.

"You wrote a list of words that describe you, but you don't know what they mean?" I questioned.

"I couldn't think of anything good about myself, so education staff helped me," Elias responded quickly. After creating a list describing the job he held in a residential facility and an outside job selling discount cards (which he described as a scam), his list of positive qualities to which we were able to add, and two volunteer projects he helped out with over the past year, Elias looked from our drafted résumé to the example résumé I had found for him online.

"Mine looks a lot smaller than theirs," he stated disappointedly.

"Do you have an email address?" I asked.

Elias grinned, "Not a professional-sounding one."

After creating a Gmail account and typing up the drafted résumé, I presented Elias with the finished product. "That's mine?" he questioned loudly. He scanned the document up and down, his eyes finally resting on the "helped prepare 800 bags of food to send overseas."

"I did that shit! I feel good about that," Elias stated proudly.

One week later, I was reading through contact notes on the computer in the control room when I came to Elias's contact notes. A note from another staff member read, "Elias requested to speak with me. He wanted to show me his new résumé and was very proud."

Two days before Elias was expected to be waived from the juvenile justice system and transferred to the county jail, I anticipated that he would be emotional and nervous when I arrived at work for my evening shift. While we were lining up after dinner, Elias asked, "Can I talk to you when we get back from dinner?"

"Sure," I responded, already expecting the request.

"Can we talk now?" Elias asked immediately when we arrived back in the multi-purpose room after dinner. Once we were settled at a table in the privacy of the West Wing, Elias began to wring his hands and look down at the floor.

"What's up?" I asked.

"I'm leaving on Monday," responded Elias, as his bottom began to stick out slightly.

"How do you feel about that?" I asked.

"I'm scared. I'm scared for my life," Elias responded, still facing the floor and beginning to rock back and forth in his chair.

As Elias and I were talking, another resident entered the unit to use the bathroom. "Bro, that little girl out there told the detention officer what we were laughing about in dining."

Elias's face immediately hardened, and anger flashed through his eyes. He glanced toward the door as if he were ready to run out and confront the resident and staff member immediately. "This is a test, Elias," I stated. "This is a chance to prove that you can keep your cool and not go off every time somebody talks about you or makes you mad."

"Yeah, but that bitch needs to keep my name out her mouth!"

he stated angrily.

"Remember when we talked about how a lot of times the bigger person walks away?" I asked.

"Yeah," Elias responded quietly.

"Are you ready to go back out there with everyone?" I asked.

"Yes."

"And you're not going to go out and confront them and escalate things when we go back out there, right?"

Elias grinned slightly and attempted to head out the door. Pulling the door shut, I stared Elias down.

"Now, if you want us to have a relationship built on trust, you can't lie to me," I reminded him.

"OK, I'm not gonna confront her. I promise," he stated.

As we walked across the multi-purpose room to the quiet room where Elias was headed, I walked next to him to attempt to create a barrier between him and the two targets of his anger. As Elias was about to enter the quiet room, he turned and glanced at the other detention officer and then again at me.

"Can I say something to her?" he asked me quickly.

"If you want to ask her to go to the other room and have a polite conversation with you, that is alright," I responded.

"Megan, can I talk to you?" he blurted out loudly in the direction of the staff member.

Megan walked over, launching into the conversation before Elias could ask to go to another room to avoid causing a scene.

"Do you have something to say to me? Because if so, you should say it to me instead of to someone else," Elias stated loudly. Megan and Elias heatedly conversed back and forth for several minutes. "You a damn liar," Elias finally concluded as he turned and entered the quiet room. I watched Elias sit and fume for a few minutes out of the corner of my eye until he waved me over. "Did I keep my promise? Did I do good?" Elias asked me quickly. "I didn't have a chance to ask her if we could talk in private," he added quickly.

"You did good," I assured him. "Aside from the 'damn liar' part at the end, you did good."

Elias smiled and nodded, satisfied. "Thank you," he remarked proudly. An hour later, the other officers and I were distributing whole wheat honey buns to the residents for snack time, when Megan took Elias's snack into the quiet room. "I'm sorry if I was rude earlier.

I didn't mean to be," Elias apologized.

The following day, Elias was in a visibly bad mood, as he knew he was likely being waived to adult court on Monday. While we were eating our meatloaf for dinner, Elias stated to the other residents, "I'm not waiting in the fucking intake room tomorrow once they waive me, and I have to wait for the sheriff to come pick me up."

I sat in silence, refusing to acknowledge Elias's statement while he was in front of his peers. However, the other detention officer in the room jumped in, explaining to Elias that he could catch charges by failing to follow instructions even after he had been waived.

"I ain't listening to nobody . . . unless Sam's here," Elias stated defiantly.

After dinner, I took Elias to make a phone call and asked if he wanted to talk once he was finished. Grinning, he nodded and joined me at a table apart from the other residents. "How are you feeling about tomorrow?" I asked him.

"I'm scared," Elias stated. "Today, the voices in my head have been real loud, telling me that if I do the things I don't wanna do just once, it will be OK. But I don't want to do that. I feel like God and the devil are fighting over me."

"You're going to be calm and behave in the morning, right? What is all this talk about refusing to wait in the intake room after court tomorrow?" I asked him.

After I explained that he could still be charged even for failing to follow detention center staff instructions after being waived to adult court, Elias declared, "Fine, I'll wait in the intake room. I ain't waiting in my JDC clothes, though. I'm gonna be wearing my street clothes."

"Be smart and follow directions, Elias," I warned him as we exited the unit.

On Monday, I checked Elias's contact notes throughout the day, determined to find out whether he behaved while being transferred from the juvenile detention center to the county jail. One contact note read, "Elias was disrespectful to the judge toward the end of court but calmed down once he was in the intake room."

Around nine-thirty that night, the county jail's phone number popped up as my phone rang loudly. "Hit 1 if you'd like to accept a call from the inmate at county jail that is trying to contact you." After I hit 1, I heard on the other line, "Sam!"

"Elias?" I questioned.

"Sam, I didn't get bond! I have to go to court before I can get it," he stated.

"Are you on the unit?" I asked.

"No, I have to spend at least twenty-four hours in intake before I can get on the unit," he responded.

"Alright, if you're there a while without bond, I'll come visit you," I assured him.

Elias was polite and sounded encouraged by the notion of having a visitor.

"Alright. Thanks for answering my call, Sam," he stated before we hung up.

As promised, I visited Elias at the facility a few days later. When he picked up the phone for our video visit, the only type allowed at the county jail, he burst into a big, lopsided grin.

"How you doing in here?" I asked him.

"I'm just chillin'," he responded.

"Now that you've been waived like you wanted, what do you think about it?" I questioned.

"Man, it's dirty as hell in here. They don't even give us underwear to wear under these things!" he exclaimed, flicking his jumpsuit sleeves. "And there ain't shit to do. We literally just walk around all day," Elias stated in shock.

"Do they have any groups in here that you can participate in?"

"No, not really, but a few guys in intake heard me talking about God in here, so they came up and asked me if I wanted to lead a prayer group with them," Elias said.

"So did you do it?" I asked.

"Yep," he responded proudly.

"Elias, you have a lot of great leadership qualities, and you could definitely use your story to help other kids when you get out of here," I encouraged him.

"You really think so?" Elias pressed, his voice full of both hope and excitement.

"For sure," I assured him.

Elias beamed.

The following week, I was at the local courthouse, attending a probation appointment with another boy involved in my organization's programming. As I paced back and forth, praying that his appointment would end before my ten-thirty appointment on the other side of town, I turned around and saw a line of men in orange jumpsuits, chained and shackled to each other, being paraded through the courthouse back to the transport van to return to the jail. I glanced over the group of men briefly when my eyes did a double-take and settled on Elias in the middle of the line.

"Elias!" I exclaimed, shocked, as I was not expecting to see him at the courthouse.

Elias simply gave me a nod, indicating that he had received bad news at court. "No talking!" the guard barked at me, conveying his great annoyance.

"Sorry," I muttered to the guard automatically, as I thought about what Elias could be feeling. When I returned home that afternoon, I checked my Telmate account to find three back-to-back messages from Elias, each message costing twenty-five cents: "I just had court the judge said no bond." "Will you come see me next week please?" "Imma call you asap."

During my next visit with Elias, his spirits seemed to be high as he chowed down on the ramen noodles he had bought at Commissary for seventy-one cents. "How are you doing?" I asked him.

"I'm alright. You know, I was reading in the Bible the other day about how God provides the right things at the right times, and I think this means I am meant to spend a few months in here because that's what will be best for me," Elias stated. "Maybe I need this time to get my stuff together."

"That's a good way to look at it," I assured him.

Halfway through my visit with Elias several days later, he confessed, "It's getting harder to stay hopeful in here without all the positive influences I had in JDC. I'm starting to lose my motivation and plans to change and all that. I know I'll still stick to my plan once I get out though," he stated.

I was unsure of whether he was more so trying to assure me or himself. "Don't worry," I told him. "We'll get you all set up when you get out of here," I did my best to assure him.

Elias shook his head and smiled.

"You know, Hector and I are helping with a homeless outreach project next Thursday. There will be lots of opportunity for you to help with things like that once you are out of here too," I stated.

"Yeah, I really wish I could be there. I can't wait to help with all that shit," Elias stated wistfully.

During my next video visit with Elias, his spirits appeared to be down slightly more than the week prior. "It's getting even harder to stay positive here," Elias conveyed. "I'm still reading my Bible every night, but I keep having these thoughts about going back to my old ways once I get out."

Elias answered my video call the following week, stating that he had been in the middle of getting a haircut. "How are things going in there?" I asked him.

"The classes are alright, but there's this one teacher in here that just pisses me off," he stated loudly.

"What do you do when she makes you mad?" I asked him.

"I mean I don't do nothing, but shit's just annoying, you know?" he replied. "Time has been going fast on the new unit," Elias explained, referencing the therapeutic unit he had requested to be transferred to within the jail. "How's the houses coming?" Elias asked in reference to the Community Change Center's reentry homes.

"They're coming along. They just take a lot of work," I told him.

"I can't wait until I'm out and can help with all that stuff," he responded. "I'm stressing in here," Elias said, his eyes looking sad and tired as he stared at the video monitor and ran his hand through his hair. "You know how I was reading the Bible every night when I got here? Lately, I've just been reading it every other night," he stated, seeming to desire some reassurance for the future.

"We'll get you in GED classes, NA, and plenty of volunteer activities when you get out," I told him. "Just focus on keeping your spirits up in the meantime."

"Am I going to see you the first day I get out?" he asked.

"Yeah, I think that would be good," I replied.

"Good. I was planning to hang out with my pops the first day I got out, but I don't think I want to do that anymore because I might get sucked into some bad stuff again," he stated. "When am I going to see you next?" Elias asked before I hung up. I promised to schedule another visit for the following week.

"What's good?" Elias asked, as he grinned when his face popped up on the video visitation screen. After asking how his buddy Hector has been doing and how the organization's renovations of its newly acquired properties were coming along, Elias's mind seemed to drift off momentarily. "My pops ain't been answering my calls for a few days," Elias commented.

"Have you tried sending him a message?" I asked.

"Yeah, I sent him a message, and he said he'd set up a visit for the next day, but then he never scheduled one. Then I called him the next day, and he said he'd schedule one again, then he didn't. And now he hasn't answered my calls for the past three days."

Sensing Elias's hurt, I asked if he had been able to talk with his mother.

"Yeah, she said she would get ahold of him. And she put money on my books since he didn't this week," he responded.

"My court date was supposed to be Monday, but they had to push it back another month 'cause of all this Corona shit," Elias stated suddenly. "I keep telling myself that it's all God's plan," Elias said quietly.

I studied Elias's expression and thought about his typical energy and excitement that was missing from his face when the "1 minute remaining of your visit" notice flashed across the screen. With the knowledge that the minute warning typically was truly a thirty-second warning, Elias asked when he would see me again.

"I'll look at my calendar and set up a visit for next week," I promised.

"Alright, take care," Elias said, attempting a smile as he hung up the phone.

During my weekly video visit with Elias, I asked how the new unit was in the jail, as the therapeutic unit had been shut down due to the current Coronavirus pandemic. Elias described the new unit as "boring as fuck." As usual, Elias asked how the demolition and construction at the organization's properties were coming and how Hector had been doing. I asked how Elias had been feeling, recognizing shifts in his language and attitude after having been in jail for several months.

"I'm alright. Just sick of being in this motherfucker!" Elias responded, describing his frustration about not having bond and having his court date pushed back due to the pandemic.

"Hey, remember it could be for a reason," I assured him.

"Yeah, I know. I've been thinking that sometimes, but sometimes I also just think this is bullshit, and I just want to get out," he stated miserably.

"Have you still been reading your Bible?" I questioned him.

"Yeah, but I haven't read it in like two days," Elias stated. "That could be something to help pass the time," I suggested. "I don't know. I've been having these thoughts," Elias stated.

"What kind of thoughts?" I asked.

"I don't even want to talk about it," Elias laughed nervously. As if on cue, the "1 minute remaining of your visit" message flashed across the screen. "Will I see you again next weekend?" Elias asked quickly.

"Yeah, if not before," I assured him.

"Alright, be safe," Elias stated, smiling as he hung up the phone.

"How's it going?" Elias asked as soon as our next weekly video call began. I could sense a dramatic change in his voice now; he sounded defeated. I asked Elias what he thought of the new unit after being there for a while.

"Now I work in the kitchen," he stated.

"How do you like working in there?" I asked.

"I don't really like it, but time goes quick as hell over here," Elias responded. "I'm finna be a cook, but they say I gotta prove myself first. She told me in like fourteen days or some shit, then I can start cooking."

"Have you talked with your family this week?" I asked.

"I talked to my mom, but she don't got nothing interesting to say, and my pops has been putting money on my shit, but he said since money is tight, he would either put money on my phone or commissary. I don't care about talking to that motherfucker, so I had him put money on my commissary," Elias explained, sounding annoyed by the thought of his parents. "And I been talking to my brother, but he don't got nothing interesting to say either. I wanna hear about somebody popping out on somebody or some drama or some shit, and all he talks about is work and his baby mama," Elias continued to complain.

As our visit neared the end, I asked if Elias had been reading his Bible.

"Nah, I ain't been reading it since I came over to this pod, like a week ago," he responded. "To be honest, I forgot all about praying."

"I think that would help. You need to get back on that," I encouraged.

"Unless God gives me some miracle, I'm not praying," Elias stated adamantly yet continued searching my face to see my response.

"See you soon," I promised as Elias smiled into the camera as the call ended.

The first week into the US lockdown due to the COVID-19 pandemic, Elias called me at nearly nine one night from the jail, which was unusual for him. "Sam? Can I ask a favor?" he immediately questioned when I answered the phone.

"What's up?" I asked him.

"I've been having a real bad headache that's got worse over the past few days, and I got a sore throat and a cough and diarrhea," he rambled quickly.

Silently panicking as he described the symptoms of COVID, I continued to listen.

"And I called my mom to ask if she'd put some money on my books, and she started freaking out. Can you put like $10 on my commissary so I can get some cough drops and shit?" he requested.

"Well, yes, I can do that, but that's not really the big issue here," I explained. "Have you gone to see the nurse and have your temperature taken or told staff that you don't feel well?" I asked.

"No, because it costs to go see the nurse, and they'll just put me in isolation if I tell them my symptoms," he replied quickly.

I asked if anyone else in the facility had been tested for the virus amidst the pandemic.

"Not that I know of, but a lot of guys on my unit are complaining of the same symptoms," Elias stated.

"Well, I'll put the money on there, but if you start to feel any worse, you need to tell someone, alright?"

"Yeah, if it gets worse, I'll tell them," he decided. "Thanks, Sam. I really appreciate it," he said before hanging up.

Elias and I continued our weekly visits until he was released a few months later. "I'll call you as soon as I get out," Elias promised the day before his release. However, it was not until approximately a year and a half later that I heard from him. While sitting at work one Friday morning, I received a Facebook Messenger request. "I need help I'm tired of fuckin around in these streets," the message said.

"It's good to hear from you! Are you free on Sunday?" I asked.

"Yes but um I just got put out where I was living I have no where to go no wants to help me I tried," he replied immediately.

When I got off work that day, I drove to pick him up with the knowledge that I could coordinate a brief respite but not long-term housing. While driving to where he would be staying, I half-jokingly told him that I had been waiting to hear from him for the past year and a half.

"I know, my bad. I was so determined to do good. Then when I got out, I just went back to all the same shit I had been doing. I got back on molly and started doing real crazy shit 'cause I was addicted. I stole from my family—from everybody—'cause all I wanted was drugs. Then I was locked up for a while again," he explained.

"What happened that time?" I asked.

"Well, it all worked out 'cause they said I was fucked up when I did what I did, and they know I wouldn't have done it otherwise. So I was facing like a level 3, and they dropped it to a level 6 for criminal recklessness."

I gave Elias my disapproving eye, but he was so caught up in his story that he didn't seem to notice. "But I've been sober since I got out of jail a month ago, and I'm ready to do good now," he stated confidently.

Without wanting to overwhelm him, I asked Elias several basic questions to help assess how difficult it would be to help him obtain gainful employment. As is a barrier for many formerly incarcerated people, Elias had been unable to work in the past due to issues with his identifying documents. Although he was a step ahead of many others in that he did have his birth certificate and social security card, he informed me that his last names did not match on the documents.

"How did that happen?" I asked him.

"Well, my dad got out of jail when I was like three, so my mom decided she would change my birth certificate to have his last name on it. Then she just never got around to changing my social security card, I guess," he stated as he rolled his eyes and looked over at me miserably.

From my experience with dealing with health departments and social security offices in the quest of obtaining identification documents, particularly during the COVID-19 pandemic when these offices were closed to the public, I knew it was likely to take several months to change the documents to reflect the same last name. Without an original, matching birth certificate and social security card, it is nearly impossible for Elias, and many others in his shoes, to obtain a state ID, which is required to be able to work a legal job.

"Well, you just rest tonight, and we'll tackle all this tomorrow," I assured him.

The following day, Elias stated that he had nowhere else to go, so he might as well accompany me to my family's big annual garage sale in Lafayette. He slept for the entire hour-and-a-half car ride there. Walking up to my cousin's big house with Elias trailing behind me as he hiked his pants up, I laughed on the inside as I braced myself for what was to come. We walked into the house and were greeted by my family as they tried their hardest to remain unfazed by the tattoos decorating Elias's face and the spiderweb tattoo covering his neck. "Nice to meet you all," he nervously said as he peeked out at them from behind me.

As the day went on, it was both comical and slightly painful to hear the interactions between Elias and my family members, who don't commonly encounter people who have lived such vastly different lives from them.

"So, what do you do?" I overheard one of my aunts ask him.

"Uh, like in the daytime?" Elias hesitated.

"Are you in school? Do you work?" she clarified innocently.

"Umm, Sam's helping me go back to school," he responded.

"So, how do you know Sam?" I heard another family member question him later.

"Uhhh, I didn't have anywhere to go yesterday, so Sam gave me a place to stay and is helping me get my life back on track," he answered matter-of-factly.

I later learned that one of my baby cousins had been questioning everyone about Elias's "face designs."

A few times throughout the day, I was reminded of the beauty, yet enormous struggle, of trying to bridge the gap between affluent, educated members of the community and those who have grown up in poverty, have a history of incarceration, and have often never even seen or experienced another way of life. One of these moments occurred when, knowing that Elias had somewhat of a spiritual background, I asked him if he wanted one of the rosaries my cousin was giving away.

"Oh, yeah, I'll take one," he responded quietly.

"You should tell them the story you told me about the rosary you found," I prodded, wanting to help make him more comfortable.

Elias lit up at the opportunity to please the group with a story.

"I was walking past this church one time, and they had this giant statue of Jesus outside," he explained, holding his arms out wide to demonstrate the size of the statue. "And he was wearing this giant rosary, and the beads were like this big." He demonstrated with his hands. "So I tried it on, and I ain't gonna lie, I stole that shit and gave it to my dad for Christmas." He laughed as my cousins' eyes grew wide, and they struggled to hold back their own laughter.

Another highlight of the day occurred when an older woman came rummaging through the garage sale items and selected a couple of large platters. "Want me to carry those to your car?" Elias asked as he jumped out of his lawn chair.

"Oh, you are so sweet. That would be great!" the woman responded.

Relieved that the woman saw Elias for who he was and had not demonstrated fear or disapproval of his tattoos, saggy jeans, or his swagger, I thought about the beauty of bridging gaps within society. I smiled as I thought about the fact that Elias had been incarcerated the previous month for battery with a deadly weapon, yet this woman was raving to her husband about how sweet he was, as Elias held her car door open for her.

Elias waited until we were alone later in the afternoon to ask his questions. "So your family just goes kayaking together, huh?" he asked, referring to some of my cousins who were leaving early to kayak down the Tippecanoe River with their youth group. "My family never did shit like that," he murmured somewhat to himself. Shortly after, as we were walking toward my car, he asked in almost a whisper, "Hey, do you think you could grab that model car off the table for me? I really want to put it together."

"You were too afraid to grab it yourself?" I asked him jokingly.

"I get shy around people, I don't know," he responded quickly.

"Are you hungry and just said you weren't because you were shy, too?" I asked.

"Yeah, I don't want to make a plate if there are other people in there," he confided.

I took him inside and told him the coast was clear; he downed two hot dogs seemingly without chewing a single bite.

As we left Lafayette, Elias attempted to put his new model car together. After a few minutes of sorting through the pieces, he decided he was better off building the model when he could sit at a table. Almost immediately after, he fell back asleep and slept the entire hour-and-a-half drive back home. Upon arriving back in town, he promptly took another two-hour nap, and I found myself wondering whether he had been staying somewhere where it was nearly impossible for him to sleep uninterrupted before.

The following morning, Elias accompanied me to church. Intrigued by a newcomer, particularly one with tattoos all over his face, the older members of the church flocked around, giving him a welcome gift and asking him to fill out a new member registration card. Elias obediently did as they asked and listened intently throughout the service. As we walked out at the end of the service, he told everyone we passed, "I'll see you next week!"

Elias spent the following Saturday helping me spray weeds, trim brush, and put together beds in one of the reentry homes still being rehabbed by my nonprofit. Knowing that the home would be utilized as transitional living for men reentering society post-incarceration once it was fully rehabbed, Elias walked into one of the bedrooms and proclaimed, "Well, somebody else is gonna have to sleep on the top 'cause I always get the bottom! That's how it was when I was in jail too!" "Can I organize the living room when it's ready?" he asked at one point, eager to help fix up the place he seemed to one day plan to live.

After completing our work at the reentry home, we drove supplies over to the church being utilized by my organization as an adult education site. I introduced Elias to the pastor of the church, who asked him if he was going to be joining our GED classes.

"Oh yeah, I'll be there," he assured the pastor.

"We hear that a lot, but we know what you're about based on what you do," the pastor preached to him.

"Oh, I'm not the same guy I used to be," Elias promised. "I'm finally ready to get my life on track."

As we left, Elias assured everyone that he would be back on Tuesday for class.

As I drove Elias to meet his brother, who had determined that they had a mutual friend Elias could stay with for the following week, I reminded him that it would be more difficult to keep on the right path if he started hanging out with the same people whom he'd gotten in trouble with in the past. I told him to call me if he became worried about his sobriety or if things got out of hand where he would be staying. He assured me that he would.

"You know, all the times I've gotten out [of incarceration] before, I always came out with goals and told myself I'd be different but then went back to the same shit that got me in trouble before. This time feels different, though. I really think I'm gonna do it," he stated as he looked toward me for assurance.

"You totally can do it," I assured him. "You just have to keep your head on straight and not go back to your old habits."

He nodded in understanding and assurance.

However, both of us knew that with nowhere stable and healthy to stay long-term, Elias would have a very difficult time turning his life around. This proved to be true, as Elias repeatedly made promises to come to class and church and then did not appear or respond to my messages in the following weeks or months. He did, however, launch a small tattoo business out of his home the following year, which I hoped would be enough of a time commitment and income generator to keep him out of trouble. Every now and again, Elias sends me a message and asks if I can help him look for work but then fails to follow through the next day. Each time, I can't help but wonder whether he reaches out in an attempt to convince me that he is still trying to get on the right track.

# CHAPTER 10

## JAVIER

While incarcerated in the local juvenile detention center at age seventeen, Javier was always very quiet and guarded. While he occasionally made a snide remark under his breath, he never caused problems and served his several months in the facility under the radar.

Nearly two years later, I was reminded of Javier when I saw his name pop up in a police report and saw his name on the local jail roster. Just a few weeks later, I observed his name on yet another police report, again for minor consumption of alcohol. Approximately two weeks later, I was walking through the local day shelter where individuals experiencing homelessness in the area frequently spend their days. Although we were all wearing masks, I stopped walking and took a second glance at one of the clients sitting at scattered tables around the center.

"Javier?" I asked.

He drew his eyebrows together and looked confused. "You look familiar," he said slowly.

I pulled my mask down and smiled.

"Oh, hey!" he said much louder. "What are you doing here?" he asked, confused.

"Just checking in on some clients. How have you been?" I responded.

"I've been better," he replied, staring at the ground. "I've seen your name in a couple of reports lately," I told him.

He looked back at me questioningly.

"You think maybe you would like to try AA?" I asked him.

"Nah, I don't know about all that,"

"Where are you staying?" I asked him.

"Uhhhhh . . . nowhere really," Javier replied slowly as his bottom lip trembled ever so slightly.

"Outside?" I asked.

Javier nodded. He was nineteen years old at the time.

Several days later, I encountered Javier at the day shelter again. "Ready for recovery services yet?" I asked him.

Javier just shrugged, seemingly out of hope for a better life.

"If I pick you up from court next week and take you to an AA meeting, will you go?" I asked him.

Javier shrugged again.

"Yes?" I questioned.

"I guess so," he said quietly.

The following Tuesday morning, I was visiting with another client at the day shelter when I noticed Javier sleeping on one of the couches, common among the shelter clients since there was no way to safely sleep outside, particularly as it grew colder outside.

"Javier," I said quietly.

When he didn't wake, I gently shook his shoulder.

"What? Oh, hi," he said as he blinked himself awake.

"Will you still come to a meeting today if I pick you up from court this afternoon?" I asked him.

"Yeah, sure. They have AA?" he asked.

"They have AA and NA," I replied.

"I think I might need that one too," he replied quickly, glancing up at me cautiously to gauge my reaction.

That afternoon, I went to the courthouse at two-thirty and headed into the D05 courtroom. Javier glanced up when I entered, and I sat on the bench in front of him. Since they were calling cases by the last name, he was at the very end of the court call. When the judge called his name, Javier, unrepresented by an attorney, walked to the gate where he was instructed to stand. The judge read off the allegations against him and asked whether he would admit or deny.

"Uhh, yeah, I did that. That's true," he stated.

The judge lowered her glasses and leaned in to get a closer look at Javier. "You're admitting?" she asked him again. "And you know how much time you could be facing if you admit today?" she pressed.

Javier stammered. "Uhhhh, no, I don't want to admit, never mind," he stuttered, clearly confused by the process.

"Alright, we'll reset for next month," the judge responded as the hearing came to a close.

"You're still going to come with me to do your intake so you can start going to meetings, right?" I asked Javier as we exited the courthouse.

"Yeah," he responded quietly. "Aren't they going to look at me and be like, 'What the fuck is this kid doing here?'" Javier worried out loud on the drive to the agency. I assured him that they had programs designed for teens, which only seemed to reassure him slightly.

When we walked in, I looked at Javier to see if he would introduce himself. He remained totally silent. "This is Javier. He's here for his three-o'clock intake," I told the staff member. Javier was escorted into a side room to discuss his substance use. As we were leaving thirty minutes later, I asked Javier how the intake went.

"It was alright, pretty standard," he replied.

As I drove Javier back to the day shelter, I asked him how work was going. Javier was an incredibly hard worker and was consistently working two jobs while experiencing homelessness at nineteen years old. Javier chuckled sadly. "I lost them both two days ago," he stated with a forced smile.

I gave him one of my infamous side glares but was more concerned than angry, as he had an impressive work ethic and great determination.

"I knew they were going to fire me after that shift, so I just quit. Well, I guess I just didn't go back, so technically, I guess I quit," he explained, clearly full of regret.

"Why did you think they were going to fire you?" I asked.

"Well, I was always high at work, but that day was different. I was just like a robot, and my boss was just looking at me like kinda disappointed but also kinda sad. So I just didn't go back," he explained.

Trying to help Javier think of other potential job options, I asked him what kind of work he would like to see himself doing long-term.

"Honestly, I don't think I'm going to live that long," he stated.

"Why do you think that?" I asked, although this was a common response among many of the young adults I worked with.

Javier grew silent before responding, "I don't know. I just don't see it."

I decided to try my hand at a little motivational interviewing for the remainder of the car ride. "What is it that you like to do?" I asked him.

"I don't know. Nothing really," Javier stated.

"What kind of work would you do if you didn't have to have any experience and there were no other barriers?" I questioned.

"Probably some kind of trade. I like to work with my hands," he ventured.

On a whim, I texted a friend of mine, Joseph, whom I knew was looking to hire a construction team at work. "Not sure if you have any use for a 19 year old with no license but he's a real hard worker haha," I texted.

"Have him call me," he responded instantly.

Javier called Joseph immediately and introduced himself.

"Can you pass a drug test?" Joseph questioned.

"Uhhhh, honestly, no, but I'm trying to get into the recovery thing," Javier replied quietly.

"Do you have time for an interview? I was about to be headed out your way anyway," Joseph stated. Less than thirty minutes later, Joseph and Javier were sitting at a local restaurant, discussing recovery, employment, and the struggles of addiction. Joseph texted me a couple of hours later.

"Where is this kid staying tonight?" he asked.

"In a tent," I responded.

"He's just sitting in a park by himself. My heart is breaking," Joseph said via text. Shortly after, Joseph called me and said he had pulled some strings and gotten Javier accepted into a local recovery home. Nearly in tears, I thanked him as I thought about the eighty people on the waitlist for the home, as well as the fact that we hadn't even submitted Javier's application to the recovery home yet.

"Are you all settled in?" I texted Javier a few hours later.

"Yes. It's really nice here," he replied. In a matter of a few hours, Javier's life changed drastically, and he knew it.

The following evening, Joseph sent me a picture of Javier asleep on the ride back to the recovery home after work. After just two days on the job, Joseph informed me that everyone at the company was so impressed by Javier and his work ethic that they gave him a $2 raise. As Javier started making more money, he began to stress about paying off legal debts so that he could begin getting his life back on track. In order to help alleviate some of his stress about his financials, I met with Javier at the recovery home to complete a budget later that week. We budgeted for him to pay off his out-of-state legal fees, which were preventing him from getting his driver's license, as well as for him to secure an attorney to fight his pending legal cases.

Once we finished the budget and I was preparing to leave, Javier mentioned that he wasn't sure how long he would last at the recovery home. With very little prodding, Javier confided in me that he had used drugs the night before. "That was pretty fucked up of me, wasn't it?" Javier stated more than asked.

After I encouraged Javier to be open and honest with the recovery home staff and others in the recovery community about what he was experiencing and continuing to use, he began speaking about his past traumas and his conscious decision to try and suppress all feelings. Nearly two hours later, I did my best to try to help Javier recap and finish the conversation feeling better than when he began talking.

"You've been through a lot. Do you think you might like having a therapist to talk with regularly to help you think through everything you just told me?" I asked.

Javier paused. "No, I don't trust anybody. I don't like to talk about my feelings," he stated adamantly. I chuckled inside as I thought about all the feelings we had just spent hours beginning to explore.

When Javier had a day off work later in the week, I picked him up at the recovery home to go to the BMV and test for his driver's license. With all his legal documents in hand, we walked into the BMV and pulled a number from the machine. As we sat in the chairs and waited, Javier rubbed his fingertips together and winced in pain. "Do you think this looks bad?" he asked as he showed me his scabbed, puffy, and likely infected fingertips. As I instructed him on how to go about treating his fingers when he got back to the recovery house, Javier thought out loud about how quickly drugs had transformed his body. "I never thought when I looked at those posters in high school that I would be that person someday. Now my teeth are all fucked up, and my fingers hurt," he pondered. Soon after, Javier's number was called, and everyone sitting near us and pretending not to overhear our conversation about meth seemed to breathe easier.

Javier approached the woman at the desk and provided his documentation. "Alright, step over here, and we'll take your picture," she told him. I watched proudly as he removed his beanie and half-smiled for his picture. "Next, you have to pass this eye exam," she told him, gesturing to the machine set up next to the desk. "Read the top line," the woman instructed him loudly. "No, the *top* line," she nearly yelled. Javier began to read again. "What? They're all letters. There's no numbers there," she stated, sounding frustrated. "Are you wearing contacts?" she asked him. Javier shook his head no. "Are you supposed to be wearing contacts or glasses?" she hollered across the desk.

"I used to have glasses, but they broke," he stated quietly.

The woman sighed. "Alright, try this line one last time," she instructed him.

Javier read the line and apparently did well enough to pass the test, and the two walked back to the woman's computer. Just as she prepared to hand all of his documentation back, she glanced back at her computer. "Apparently, you have some things you need to clear up in Ohio before we can allow you to test for your license," she stated. She handed Javier a paper with the Ohio BMV's contact information listed. "Call them and get that taken care of, and then you can come back," she instructed him.

Clearly disappointed, Javier walked back to where I was sitting. "Nothing can ever be easy," he sighed.

"What happened in Ohio?" I asked him.

"I'm not even really sure. I got an OWI or some shit out there a few years ago," he stated sadly.

"Well, give them a call this afternoon, and we'll get it figured out," I assured him. As I drove him back to the halfway house, we made a to-do list, which Javier diligently began working on as soon as we walked in the door of the home.

Just two days later, Joseph texted me that Javier had been kicked out of the recovery home for using drugs. He informed me that he tested positive for heroin, cocaine, and a handful of other substances. I checked my work phone and saw that Javier had texted me, "LMAO that didn't last long." A woman with a heart for the guys at the recovery home invited Javier to stay with her and her family so that he wouldn't be back sleeping in the woods in the cold weather. Javier continued showing up for work in the following days, although he refused to say whether or not he was actively using. Every few days, Joseph texted me to tell me how impressed the company was with Javier's work and that they were giving him additional pay raises as a result. While talking with Javier on the phone one afternoon about his case management updates, he stated, "Apparently, the company is really happy with my work. Joseph says I could have a career here, and I don't want to mess that up. Hopefully, that is enough to keep me sober."

One morning a few weeks later, Joseph texted me that Javier would be returning to the halfway house after work that day. "That's great! What made him change his mind about being ready to stay sober?" I responded.

"Idk, sometimes it just takes time," Joseph texted back. As planned, Javier moved back into the halfway house later that day. I continued to periodically check in on him, following up after court hearings and making sure he remembered his doctor appointments.

Javier continued striving to improve himself and his life. Joseph informed me one day that Javier asked him to be his sponsor, indicating his readiness to actively work toward maintaining his sobriety. I texted Javier to tell him I was proud of him and encouraged him to keep making "big moves," as he and I often call his successes.

"Thank you. What do you think my next big move should be?" he asked.

We talked about the importance of paying off the lawyer he had hired to handle the criminal cases he picked up while he was still using drugs, as well as his progress toward obtaining his driver's license, buying a car, and eventually renting his own apartment. I assured him that those were enormous successes and would be plenty for him to work on for the next few months.

One Saturday morning in the middle of February, I picked Javier up from the halfway house where he was still staying. Moments after I texted him to let him know I was parked out back waiting on him, Javier hopped into my passenger seat with a smile on his face. As we drove to a nearby coffee shop to catch up, Javier brought me up to speed regarding the 180-degree shift his life had taken over the past few months. A self-proclaimed Satanist, Javier said he had been going to church with the woman who housed him when he was kicked out of the halfway house but that he was going to tell her he didn't want to go anymore since he doesn't believe in God.

We walked into the coffee shop, and the barista asked Javier what he would like. "Do you think they have Americanos?" he asked.

"I'm sure they do," I told him.

"I'll have an Americano with an espresso shot in it, please," Javier said to the barista.

"Joseph got you hooked on those too, huh?" I smiled as I asked Javier.

He smiled and nodded. We spent the next hour and a half discussing Javier's job, new medical insurance, plans for buying his own car soon and eventually renting an apartment, and wisdom teeth. He also proudly showed me a video on his phone of a mouse stuck in the window well at the halfway house. When Javier told me about his new credit card, I expressed the importance of not spending more on it than he would be able to pay off each month. "I know, I know. I can see the worry in your eyes," Javier laughed. "I only buy little drinks and food at the gas station on it so I can start building my credit."

At ten minutes before nine, I asked Javier if he wanted me to drop him off at home or if he wanted to go to church with me. I was surprised when he shrugged and said, "Sure, I'll go."

Javier was scheduled to work a shift at a local pizza restaurant at ten-thirty, where he was working three shifts per week to save up additional money, so we determined that I would take him back to the halfway house to change into his work clothes before work and then drive him to the restaurant across town for his shift.

Javier and I went to church, and as we were walking through the parking lot after the service, Javier smiled and said, "Can I drive?"

Knowing that he likely did need driving practice before he went to take his driving test the following weekend, I agreed. I hardly took a breath as I tried to sit calmly while Javier pulled jerkily out of the parking lot.

"Woah, this thing is sensitive," Javier remarked. "Can I drive to work?" he asked, grinning as he pulled into the halfway house driveway. Javier changed clothes quickly and came back out, pleased to be sliding back into the driver's seat. We discussed Ivy Tech's Next Level Jobs program and what certificate program he might be interested in completing as he drove. When we came to a red light at a right turn, Javier remained stopped at the light even with no other cars in sight.

"Did you know you can turn right on red as long as there are no cars coming and there's no sign that says, 'No turn on red?'" I asked.

"Huh, nope, didn't know that," he replied as he turned. A few minutes longer into the drive, I worried out loud whether he would forget that you can only turn *right* on red.

As we sat at a red light through which he needed to drive straight, Javier said, "So I can go now, right?"

I turned to look at him in disbelief when I saw he was grinning. Javier pulled into the restaurant parking lot and hopped out to readjust the seat to where it was before he had to adjust it for himself. "Have a good shift!" I told him.

"You too," he replied.

"Errrrr, I mean, have a good day!" He laughed as he walked inside.

Just several weeks later, I was walking across town running errands when I heard someone yell my name. I turned and saw Javier standing in the parking lot next to a giant black truck. "You look all fancy," he stated.

"Yep, I have to dress up a little bit for work," I acknowledged before asking whose truck he was driving.

"This is mine," Javier said proudly. "I just got it this week."

Overwhelmed by disbelief and my pride in this nineteen-year-old kid, I told him how impressive the truck was and how even more impressive he was. Looking at the clock on my phone, I reminded Javier that he better go check in with his probation officer before he was late, as his 10:00 a.m. appointment was the reason he was not at work that morning.

Less than a month later, Javier texted me, "Guess what." I did not have any good guesses. "I got into the Laborers Union," he replied. He explained the training process to get started with his official apprenticeship, and I asked how he was feeling about all of it. "Proud," he replied simply. "You should be," I responded.

Several weeks later, I texted Javier to see if he wanted to have lunch and catch up. On the day of our lunch, he told me about the various jobs he had been working through the Union, his search for his own apartment, the strategies he had been using to build his credit, and how mad he was being required to go to counseling as a term of his probation. As we finished eating and the waitress brought the bill, Javier quickly snatched it up before I could give her my card. Less than ten days later, I received a call from Javier, during which he told me he would be moving into his first, very own apartment in a couple of days.

On the day of his move, I met him at the men's day shelter where they knew him from the days he would wander in for a sandwich when he didn't have anything to eat. We walked around their resale shop picking out pots, pans, end tables, lamps, and other basics for his apartment. The shelter gifted all of the materials to him, and the staff raved about his ability to take advantage of the opportunity he had been given and completely change his life around. After dropping off the materials at his apartment, we purchased a mattress and bedframe and returned to his new apartment to begin unpacking. After setting up his bed, arranging the few end tables he had, and placing the donated pots, pans, and other assorted kitchen supplies on the kitchen floor to be washed once he bought a pack of sponges, I glanced around the apartment. He had his work tools proudly lined up against the wall in the living room. One ancient looking floor lamp was the only piece of furniture in the kitchen. I smiled and assured Javier that almost everyone starts out eating on the floor when they move into their first apartment. As I handed him the list of cleaning supplies and assorted household materials he still needed to buy, I told Javier that he should have a move-in picture to remember the day. Although he protested, he eventually smiled long enough for me to snap a picture of him standing proudly in the middle of his empty living room.

"I'm very proud of you," I told him as I hugged him goodbye.

*Javier in his very first apartment*

Knowing that 19-year-old Javier would be unlikely to stock his kitchen in a way that I felt was healthy, I dropped off a big box of food to him a few days later.

"Be sure to put all this milk in the fridge as soon as I leave," I warned him as he laughed. As I was driving home just fifteen minutes later, Javier texted me a picture of the groceries in his now fully stocked fridge.

"Thank you so much Sam. I'm gonna love you forever," he texted.

Several weeks went by, during which I heard from Javier sporadically. During one humorous call, he asked why his new shower curtain didn't come with any rings.

"Uh you just have to feel around in the package and see whether the rings are included," I explained. I held back laughter as he roared back, "Why didn't they tell me that at the store then?!"

A month and a half after Javier moved into his apartment, I woke up to a text from him one morning that said, "Im sorry sam." My heart sunk to the ground, and I immediately texted back to ask what was wrong. When I still hadn't heard back from him an hour later, I texted again to ask if he was safe. "Im okay," he replied. After a little bit of prodding to find out why he felt the need to apologize to me at 2:30 in the morning, Javier stated that he had a bad night and was sorry that he thought he had let me down. I asked him to meet me at the local church the next day where I host a community meal every Friday evening. Javier agreed to attend the community dinner the following day so we could chat about what happened, but he did not show up at the dinner.

The following week, Javier called me while I was out having dinner with a friend. Fairly confident that he was using again, I answered the phone to ensure he was alright. A very paranoid Javier rapidly explained to me why he thought he was going to jail and how he had been set up. After confirming that he was safe for the night, I again asked him to meet up with me the following day so we could chat. Although he agreed, I did not hear from Javier for a couple more days until he called me and confided in me that he thought he was going to lose his Union job. While he wouldn't go into detail over the phone about what had happened, I was watching his life quickly unravel around him. I told him that if he decided he would agree to go to treatment, I would connect him with detox services immediately.

The following Monday evening, I was at home preparing my weekly curriculum for the reentry group I run in a local prison, when Javier called. Knowing that something bad had to be happening for Javier to call me at 9:00 p.m., I answered the phone.

"I'm ready to come back to the land of the living," Javier said quietly. He explained that he had made a series of very poor choices, his truck had broken down, and he had walked off a job site and been suspended at work, and now he was sitting at the local grocery store with no gas and an overheated truck. "I went through my whole phone list. I really didn't want to have to call you," he moaned quietly.

I met Javier at the store and walked up to his truck. Upon seeing a young woman with blue hair, who did not look up from her phone as I approached the truck and began talking with Javier, I recognized that he was in a much worse situation than I had previously expected. He hopped out of the truck, and his loose jeans and baggy sweatshirt showed that he had lost at least twenty-five pounds in less than two months. Javier leaned his head against his truck as it filled with fuel, and then he seemed to forget where we were.

"How do I keep from using tonight?" he asked, somewhat rhetorically.

"Do we need to go inside and buy coolant?" I asked him gently.

"Yeah, I would appreciate it," Javier responded as he hung his head low.

After filling the truck up with coolant, I asked Javier to come sit in my car and chat, away from the woman in his truck.

I explained to him that if they are using drugs together and he intends to stop using, he would need to distance himself from her.

"I was trying to help her," he explained as his lip began to quiver. "I told her this morning that we should go to an NA meeting, but she wouldn't go so I didn't go either. Really I think that I just knew that I needed one," he said as tears began to run down his face.

Javier explained that he sees that he worked hard to get to where he was and that he is so afraid to lose it all. I pointed out that he hadn't yet lost his job, his vehicle, or anything else that he has been working to establish. However, I informed him that it seemed like he very well could lose those things if he chose not to seek treatment. For the next two hours, Javier cried, paused every so often and asked if the voices he was hearing were real, and went back and forth debating about whether he needed treatment.

As the time neared 11:15 p.m., the woman who had been sitting in Javier's truck texted him to ask if they could leave. After I encouraged him to let her know that he wouldn't be able to house her for the night, he went to drive her back to the drug-filled house where she was staying. Because Javier was afraid he would take a detour to buy meth on the way back to his apartment, I told him I would wait for fifteen minutes in the gas station parking lot so he could drop her off and I could follow him home. At nearly 11:45 p.m., Javier returned to the gas station so I could follow him back to his apartment and ensure that he arrived safely and without purchasing drugs.

When we arrived at his apartment, we stood in the parking lot, and I again explained to Javier that treatment might be critical if he wanted to beat the disease. He expressed his concern that he would be fired for missing too much work and that it is embarrassing to ask for help. Finally, we decided we would continue the conversation the following day. After learning that Javier had nothing but a carton of eggs to eat in his house, I loaded him up with an armful of shrimp Ramen that I always keep in my trunk.

"Thank you," he called out miserably as he walked slowly toward his apartment door. Less than an hour later, my phone rang again as I was finally sliding into bed. Seeing that it was Javier calling and fearing that the likelihood of him using and dying that night would increase if I did not pick up, I answered the phone.

"Are the noises I'm hearing real?" he asked.

I assured him that the noises were in his head and that he needed to eat his Ramen and get some sleep. Seeming to feel better, Javier agreed and hung up the phone.

The following afternoon at nearly 3:15pm, Javier called again. "I just woke up!" he exclaimed, sounding like he was holding back tears. As he had supposed to be at a worksite to redeem himself and keep his job that morning at 6:30, he was understandably angry with himself. "I set 10 alarms and don't understand how I just slept through every single one of them," he cried. I pointed out the fact that there was nothing else he could do to fix the situation in the moment and encouraged him to go do something healthy since he had the afternoon off of work. We brainstormed prosocial activities together, such as going for a walk, going to the music shop to play the guitars, and cleaning his apartment, and Javier agreed to catch an NA meeting at 7:00 p.m. that evening.

Just after 7:30 p.m., I was once again having dinner with a friend when Javier called in a panic. "I showed up at the NA meeting listed on my app just now, but it was only for women! Then I drove to another one that was listed but I can't even find it!" he exclaimed. Looking at the clock and confirming online that he had already missed the local NA meetings for the night, I texted him a link to recorded testimonials that are shared widely through Celebrate Recovery meetings. I also texted Javier's old sponsor and pleaded with him to reach out to Javier and see how he is doing. His former sponsor texted back and informed me that Javier was on his way to his house right then, immediately providing me with a sense of relief.

The following morning, I woke up to a message from Javier saying he used the night before and he was sorry but he got back into 'that' mindset. I told him that there was no need to apologize to me but that he did need to go to treatment. After seeing that Javier read a few of my messages encouraging detox without responding, I finally called his phone. Javier explained that he had driven to the wrong worksite that morning and his boss said he would give him one very last chance. "I was seriously considering going to treatment until they said they would let me come back to work," he stated. I encouraged him again to come to the church where I would be volunteering at that afternoon.

Javier did arrive at the church, although he was a couple hours late. We completed a rental assistance application for the township trustee's office and talked for another hour about how embarrassed he is to ask for assistance. I reminded him of the group of people that care about him, and he responded that he wished he was a less selfish person so he could truly appreciate that. As Javier continued to deny going to detox, I sent him with four bags of beef stew and encouraged him to call me when he was ready for treatment.

A couple Fridays later, I was preparing dinner at the Unity Cafe where I serve community dinners on Friday, when Javier appeared around the corner with a big grin on his face. I told him it was good to see him and asked if he was able to stay for dinner, to which he agreed. Javier helped me set up dinner as we debated the pros and cons of going to detox. Javier explained that he didn't want to lose his apartment by going, to which I explained that he was inevitably going to lose much more than his apartment if he did not go to treatment. I pulled on my plastic gloves to begin serving dinner, and Javier asked if he could help serve as well. As he plated baked spaghetti and garlic bread for everyone who came through the line, Javier seemed to feel a sense of peace. After everyone was served and we had both eaten as well, Javier asked how I got into social work. He talked about how he feels guilty that he is choosing to destroy his life when there are people like those at the Cafe who "really need help." I reminded him that addiction is a disease and that it makes us do uncharacteristic things and act like people we are not.

Later in the week, Javier excitedly told me that he had a second interview at Aldi coming up and that he was fairly confident he would get the job. I confirmed that he had a bike available to ride to the interview and told him to let me know how the interview went. Javier called me the afternoon of the interview and frantically told me that he left his apartment on his bike with plenty of time to stop at the gas station, change shirts, and arrive to the interview early, but somehow time went faster than expected and he arrived late at the interview. After acknowledging his frustration and disappointment, I reminded Javier that it is really difficult to function normally when using drugs and again encouraged him to go to treatment so he would be able to obtain and keep a job. Javier thanked me for listening and hung up.

Several days later, Javier texted me to ask whether applying for SNAP would affect his taxes next year. I did not hear from him for several days afterwards, until he texted me at 7:00 a.m. one morning asking if I had a minute to talk. Expecting him to be in deeper legal or financial trouble and wanting to process it with me, I called him already prepared for bad news.

"I'm ready for recovery and want to apologize to you for declining your help for so long," he started. "It was a really bad night, and I'm on my way to see my probation officer to lay everything on the table," he stated.

He told me that he still wasn't sure whether he wanted to go to detox but that he knew something had to change in order for him to survive. Avoiding jail time by going to treatment would also serve as an incentive, depending upon what his probation officer said. I encouraged him to call me after he spoke with his probation officer.

Later that Friday afternoon, Javier called me and told me he would be leaving for inpatient treatment on Tuesday. He sounded relieved as he described the bills he needed to shut off, etc. before leaving for treatment. I told him I was proud of him and invited him to come to the Unity Cafe that evening for dinner. Ten minutes before the Cafe was set to close that night, Javier texted me and asked if there was any extra food. I called him and asked whether he was already on his way or if he was planning to walk there from his apartment across town and arrive at 9:00 p.m., an hour after the Cafe closes.

"I'll ride my bike there . . . and make it at 9," he laughed.

I told him I would just drop a plate off at his apartment once I locked up the building.

I arrived at Javier's apartment with the leftover food, and we sat at the table to look at his bills and a letter regarding a court hearing which he did not understand. We discussed how he was feeling about going to treatment, and he worried out loud about all the people he had hurt. Javier pointed toward a bike that was sitting in the kitchen which appeared to be substantially damaged.

"I let one of my buddies ride it, and he brought it back like this," he stated sadly as he shook his head. "You should have seen Gina's face when she saw it," he murmured, referring to a woman who had taken him into her family and been allowing him to sleep on her couch and helping him out for the past year.

"She gave me one, and I ruined it so she gave me this one." He shook his head again. Javier blinked back tears as he said that someone can only love you so much before they give up on you. We talked about how his family abandoned him and why that didn't have to mean that everyone in his life would leave him. Javier, eyes filled with tears, talked about the day when his grandma dropped him off at the courthouse with a backpack and said he was no longer welcome at her house, never speaking to him again.

"You didn't deserve that, Javier," I stated quietly as he began to cry.

He explained that he was terrified to be at his apartment alone over the weekend, as his drug-induced psychosis caused him to see and hear things that weren't there. As if on cue, Gina called him. I watched his face light up as he described to her the happenings of the day and his commitment to going to treatment on Tuesday. Javier finally asked Gina if he could stay at her house that evening and over the weekend until he went to treatment. As it was already nearly 10:00 p.m., Gina told him that he could definitely stay Saturday and Sunday night, but that it was probably too late in the evening for him to stay with her and her family that night. Javier thanked her, hung up the phone, and looked at me with fear and sadness all over his face.

"I don't know that I can let you stay all night, but would you feel better if you came to my house for a while so you aren't here by yourself?" I asked.

"Yes, I would feel better. Thank you," he stated quickly. "Do you want me to wear long sleeves?" Javier asked, glancing at the track marks on his arms as he gathered a few of his belongings to bring with us.

As we drove to my house, Javier mentioned that he had been unable to pee normally for days and that it hurt when he could. I asked if he had been drinking water, to which he replied that he was not sure but doubted it. Back at my house, Javier quietly sat at my kitchen table and ate while he watched my partner and foster son play video games. Shortly after, my boyfriend, Aric, slid into the chair across from Javier and asked him about himself. They talked for nearly an hour before Javier suddenly tensed up, gripping the sides of the chair tightly with his head down, and clenching his teeth. When he remained in the position for nearly thirty seconds, I grew concerned and walked over to him, realizing he had a leg cramp. I helped him onto the floor and filled a glass of water. Once the cramp finally passed, Javier drank three glasses of water and continued to chat with us about his life, his aspirations, and how terrified he was to lose his life to his disease.

At nearly midnight, Gina decided it would be alright for Javier to stay with her family overnight and came to pick him up. As he gathered his belongings, I reminded Javier how proud of him I was and told him he would be welcome to come with us to the Fourth of July festival at the lake over the weekend if he would like. I reminded him to drink lots of water as he headed out the door with the cup of water I sent with him.

The following morning, Javier texted me to ask if Aric could help him move his belongings out of his apartment over the weekend. I told him that we would be out of town over the weekend but could definitely help move him out on Monday, as it was a holiday, and we were all off work. On Monday morning, Aric and I showed up at Javier's apartment to find Gina and Javier boxing up kitchen supplies and moving around the few pieces of furniture which he had accumulated. While Gina and I were able to store the small belongings for him, neither of us had room for his bed frame, mattress, the recliner that Javier and I had previously acquired from the side of the road, or kitchen table. With nowhere to store his belongings and with the knowledge that he would be leaving for treatment for a month the following day and was nearly $2,500 in debt to the apartment complex, we piled up all the furniture by the dumpster outside.

As Aric, Javier, and I pulled away from the complex in my car, I looked at Javier in the backseat and saw pain, embarrassment, and disappointment written all over his face.

"This is a new chapter. The only thing that matters is that you're alive," I stated.

Javier shook his head weakly.

"Let's all jump in the pool," I stated as we pulled past the complex's pool on our way out. Javier looked up and grinned. I pulled the car over, and we greeted the two men who were sitting by the pool, kicked off our shoes, and jumped in the water. Five minutes later, we were all sopping wet in the car.

"That was the sendoff I needed," Javier stated, smiling from the backseat.

We picked up my foster son at my house and headed out of town for the festival. Javier and my foster son took turns picking which songs to play via Bluetooth all the way to the festival. Once we arrived, they both enjoyed burgers, corn dogs, cheese fries, and a fried twinkie. Javier laughed, joked, and seemed to almost feel like he could let his guard down and just be taken care of for a day. After the festival, we all went swimming at a friend's house, and I watched with a full heart as Javier and my foster son talked, smiled, and pet the friend's dog after we completed all of our races and handstand competitions in the pool.

Forgetting that all the restaurants downtown would be closed for the Fourth of July holiday, we made what seemed to be a pointless trip downtown. However, I did not take for granted the lighthearted conversations or jokes that Javier made as we walked. Instead, I said a prayer of gratitude that he was alive to see another day.

After finishing off two Casey's pizzas for dinner instead of the sit-down restaurant meal we had hoped for, we walked to the fairgrounds to enjoy the fireworks. As we were sitting on our blanket in the grass awaiting the show, the announcer played some jazzy music on the speakers. Javier talked about how much he missed playing the saxophone and reminisced on playing solos in every band concert possible when he was in high school. He lamented the fact that he had to choose between taking his guitars or taking his saxophone— and deciding on the guitars when he was kicked out of his parents' home at nineteen.

As we were driving home after fireworks, Javier was quiet until he remarked, "You know, a lot of people say they had to have one more "good one" before they go to rehab. They have to use one last time, and they have to go all out. Today was way better than that."

The following day, I asked Javier how he was feeling about leaving for inpatient treatment. He responded that he was still feeling excited, but that the facility's cab was no longer able to pick him up until the following day. Thankfully, Gina and her family allowed him to stay at their home an extra night. The day after, Javier texted me in the afternoon and let me know that he was on his way to treatment.

"Proud of you," I responded.

# Chapter 10

# Lamar

While I was helping out at a local adult education class one evening, I received a call from the director of the men's shelter down the road. "I have a young kid here, Lamar, who would like to earn his GED," he stated.

"You can bring him on by tonight if he's free!" I told him, always happy to enroll new students into the program. Thirty minutes later, the director dropped off a young boy, no more than 120 pounds, completely swallowed by his winter jacket and carrying a big, dirty backpack. I welcomed the boy and explained the program. "Do you want to get enrolled and start pretesting tonight?" I asked him.

Lamar shrugged. "I ain't got nothing better to do," he stated.

After class, I drove Lamar back to the men's shelter. "I gotta get myself out of this situation. I don't wanna end up like the people I seen this morning smoking crack outside the gas station," he stated matter-of-factly as he stared out the window. "I've messed up a lot, and that's why my mom left me at this shelter, but I feel like I'm getting on the right track now," he assured both of us. When I dropped Lamar off outside the shelter, I handed him my business card. "You call me if you need anything. We'll see you at class tomorrow."

"Definitely. Thanks for the ride," he replied as he slid out of the car.

Knowing that Lamar had aged out of the foster care system and that Indiana has an extended foster care program that provides former foster youth with financial assistance if they qualify for the program, I called the Department of Child Services the following morning. I provided his information to the hotline worker, and a caseworker from the Older Youth Services (OYS) program in the region met with him at the adult education classes just a few days later to complete his intake. They explained the program to Lamar and me, stating that as long as he attended his case management meetings and engaged with his caseworker, they would help him financially and obtain a three-year housing voucher for him.

As the caseworker and her supervisor were preparing to leave after completing the intake, the supervisor stated, "Now that you're in this program, we will make sure that you don't ever have nowhere to stay at night. If you find yourself without anywhere to go, even if it's two in the morning, you call us." Amazed by all the program was able to offer, I stressed to Lamar the importance of keeping his case management appointments after the caseworker left.

Lamar attended the adult education class consistently for the next couple of weeks. In the evenings, when I was helping out with the class, I would give him a ride back to the shelter afterward. One evening after class, Lamar informed me that he had left the shelter and was staying with a friend nearby instead. When I pulled up to drop him off at his friend's apartment, I quickly noticed the broken glass all over the street and the fact that the apartment complex didn't appear habitable. "Are you sure you are safe here?" I asked Lamar.

"Safe enough," he shrugged as he closed the car door.

A couple of days later, I awoke in the morning to a text from Lamar, sent at 3:00 a.m.: "Help gotta get out of here."

"Are you safe now?" I texted back. I didn't hear back from Lamar until later that evening, as he didn't have service on his phone and, therefore, could only use it while on Wi-Fi.

"I can't go back there," he texted.

With the caseworker's words in my head, I was confident that the OYS providers would be able to house him somewhere if I went and picked him up. Lamar told me where he was, and I drove to make sure he was safe and help him call the DCS hotline. I pulled up to his friend's house and texted Lamar that I was outside. He immediately came out of the apartment complex and hopped in the car. As I observed the deep scratches across his face, I asked him what had happened.

"He just started acting real dumb last night, and we got in a fight, then he pulled out a gun," he explained.

I suggested he try to go back to the shelter he had chosen to leave a few days prior. "They told me I couldn't come back since I left for two nights, but I guess we can try," he stated quietly.

"Did you eat today?" I asked Lamar. He shook his head no, so we stopped for a pepperoni pizza at Little Caesars and then proceeded to the shelter. I pulled up at the shelter and instructed him to walk in, already apologizing for leaving. He came back out no more than fifteen seconds later, shaking his head.

"They just looked at me and immediately said no," he stated. We sat in the car while I dialed the DCS hotline number and asked for the OYS supervisor to call us.

Aware that it was a Sunday evening and nobody would be prepared to be working or find a bed for a twenty-year-old with nowhere to go, I drove us to my apartment while we waited on a callback. Nearly two hours later, the OYS supervisor finally called. When I explained what had happened, the supervisor sounded stressed as she explained that they could try to find a hotel where he could stay for the night, but they weren't sure if they would even accept him since he wasn't twenty-one. Sensing the stress and lack of a plan for him, I offered to allow him to stay at my house overnight so they could formulate a better long-term plan for him the following day.

In the morning, I drove Lamar to the OYS office, where we explained what happened and why he now had no housing options. I offered to call the director of the shelter he had not been permitted to return to the previous evening to see if he could possibly go back to stay there if he promised not to stay out overnight again. When I called the director, he explained that they have a rule against allowing people to come back after they do not report back to the shelter at night but determined that they would make an exception for Lamar this one time. The OYS caseworker drove Lamar back to the shelter that afternoon, and we believed all was settled.

A few days later, I happened to be at the shelter to meet with the director to talk about a project we were collaborating on. He asked how Lamar was doing and whether he was still attending class.

"What, he hasn't been here?" I asked in disbelief.

"I thought you knew! He left the same day that caseworker brought him back here," he explained. I shook my head, at a loss for words.

When I left the shelter, I drove to the adult education classes down the road, where I found Lamar standing outside the door, smoking a blunt.

"Why did you leave the shelter, and why are you smoking weed right outside my class?" I asked him.

Lamar shrugged.

"Get rid of that and come inside so we can talk," I stated sharply.

Lamar obliged and came walking slowly into the classroom.

"Why did you leave the shelter again?" I asked him.

"The guys don't like me there, and it's boring as hell," he complained. "I didn't even do nothing to them, and they start talking 'bout I'm gonna get kicked out 'cause I shine my flashlight when I'm getting ready for work at five in the morning. They said I don't make my bed right and all kinds of shit, and I got tired of it," he said, getting more and more worked up.

"What makes you think it's going to work out at your friend's this time?" I asked.

Lamar explained that they talked through it, and he just had to lie low until he could get his own place.

Just two days later, I checked my phone on Sunday afternoon to find three missed calls, a voicemail, and several frantic texts from Lamar stating that he was getting shot at and asking if I could come and pick him up. Very frustrated at this point but even more aware of the help he needed, I drove to pick him up. After OYS's lack of placement options the previous Sunday evening when I called the hotline, I took Lamar back to my house again and texted the caseworker that I had him with me and could keep him until they figured out a better plan the following day.

The next morning, I dropped Lamar off with his caseworker so they could create a housing plan for him. A couple of hours later, she called me and asked if I would be willing to be a host home, essentially a foster home with significantly less financial reimbursement and less strict requirements. I agreed to house Lamar until we could obtain his housing voucher and move him into his own apartment.

Very quickly, I learned about the very unfair deck of cards Lamar had been dealt. Most of his family was incarcerated, aside from his mother, who was also experiencing homelessness. Lamar frequently struggled with how to respond to his mother's constant Venmo requests for money and the fact that she kept his social security check each month. When asked why he always gives her the money, even when he knows it is his last few dollars, Lamar stated, "She's my momma. I don't want her to go without." Lamar also struggled with serious mental illness himself, making it even more difficult for him to function appropriately and leading to his brief hospitalization within the first few weeks of the host home placement.

Aside from listening to teenage drama over FaceTime and the occasional loud music, the host home arrangement went relatively smoothly until one morning, I walked into the house after having been at the grocery store and was greeted by the smell of a marijuana cloud. I waited until we were loaded up in the car, headed to church, and then turned to face Lamar.

"Is it me, or does it smell like weed in the house?" I asked him.

Lamar was silent for a minute before slowly replying, "Uh, it might smell a little bit like weed."

After explaining the ramifications of being caught with marijuana in a state where it is still illegal, Lamar assured me that he understood. He slowly pulled his lighter out of his pocket, rolled down the car window, and tossed out the marijuana he had hidden inside the cap. "Alright, it's gone, no more," he assured me.

That morning at church, the pastor spoke about generosity and tithing. At the end of the service, Lamar quietly slipped his last few dollars into the collection box at the door.

One evening several weeks later, I noticed Lamar was outside for a suspicious amount of time. I opened the front door and was immediately met with an overwhelming scent of marijuana. "I know you are *not* smoking on this porch," I said loudly.

Lamar looked up at me as if he were about to burst into tears. He looked down at the ground and then back up as he remained seated on the porch chair. "It's gone now," he stated, sounding defeated.

"This isn't going to work, Lamar. I told you that you can't do this here." I shook my head and shut the door.

The following morning, Lamar and I hopped in the car for our normal routine of dropping him off at the local library to apply for jobs and work on schoolwork while I went to work. "You remember I told you that you can't smoke here, right?" I asked him as I drove toward the library.

"Yeah," he replied. "So why did you decide to smoke on the porch last night?"

"I just wanted to relax, and I guess I didn't feel like walking farther away to do it," he stated.

"Well, because it's still illegal in Indiana, you risk my housing, and therefore your housing, and my job, when you smoke here," I explained. "So you understand that if it happens again—if I see it, smell it, anything—you can't stay with me anymore," I stated.

"Yeah, I understand," he replied.

"Alright, have a good day," I hollered out the car door as I dropped him off at the library.

That evening, I was reminded of the humor of housing young males as I lay in bed while Lamar watched TV in the living room. Suddenly I heard clear as day, "Siri, what is no-nut November?"

By the following Sunday, Lamar seemed to be doing well as he worked on math homework in the living room and completed job applications online. He attended church with me, and only once did I have to scold him when he began rapping out loud in the middle of the pastor's sermon. The next morning, as usual, I went to open his bedroom door to make sure he was up and getting ready so that we could leave on time. That morning, the door seemed to be blocked. I managed to push it open and looked behind the door to see what had been preventing it from opening smoothly. I noticed the purple towel rolled up against the door.

"Are you kidding me?" I asked as Lamar woke up groggily. As I glanced around, I suddenly realized how cold it was in the room and noticed both of his windows were open. "Do you think I was born yesterday?" I questioned loudly as I slammed the windows shut and found a hollowed-out mechanical pencil jammed with a ball of wax on the windowsill. "We're leaving in twenty minutes," I stated as I grabbed the pencil and walked out of the room. Lamar silently got up and dressed. When he walked into the kitchen where I was making my coffee to go, he tried to feel out what I was thinking without asking.

"What time do you think I should call Walmart to follow up on my job application there?" he asked, sounding too upbeat and eager.

"Just wait until after 9:00 a.m.," I replied as my mind reeled, knowing that I would have to find somewhere else for him to stay.

"You sound depressed," he stated quietly, making the statement sound like somewhat of a question, pretending he didn't know why I might be upset.

I dropped him off at the library, as usual, and called his case manager to explain the situation.

OYS's case manager was able to use some of the money allotted toward his housing to put him in a hotel room while we looked for another shelter that would accept him. I called the shelter he had not been permitted to return to previously, yet they said they did not want him to return since he had smoked marijuana in the doorway of their facility as well. The following day, the hotel manager called Lamar's caseworker and informed her that he could not return to the hotel since they found paraphernalia in the bathroom of his room. After some pleading on Lamar's behalf and with the acknowledgment that he would be charged a $250 fine if he smoked in the room again, the hotel agreed to allow him to return for one more night.

The following day, the caseworker and I were able to get Lamar into the only other overnight shelter for men in the area. After helping complete his intake, I went into the locker room to help Lamar learn how to work the combination on his lock.

"Are you alright?" I asked him once we were alone.

A single tear rolled down his cheek. The shelter staff came into the room to provide him with additional info about the rules and procedures of the shelter, and Lamar quickly wiped his eyes. We walked to the front of the building to say goodbyes as his caseworker and I prepared to leave. Lamar sat in a chair, pulled his hood up as far as he could, and fixed his gaze on his phone while his bottom lip trembled slightly.

"Alright, Lamar, we're leaving now, but you know you can text or call us at any time, right?"

Lamar nodded while tears began streaming down his face, and he pulled his hood even farther over himself.

Just three days later, the manager of the overnight shelter texted me that Lamar reeked of weed and, therefore, could no longer stay at the shelter. Exasperated but not surprised, I texted his caseworker and arranged to meet with the shelter manager when I was finished with my next meeting at work. I arrived at the shelter just a couple of hours later and walked inside. I called Lamar into the manager's office, and the three of us sat down.

"Why do you think I'm here, Lamar?" I asked softly.

He shrugged.

"What happened last night?" I tried again.

"I don't know," he stated, halfway glancing at me while trying to keep his eyes focused on the floor.

"Did you smoke last night, Lamar?" I asked more forcefully.

"Uhhhhhhhh," he hesitated.

"Honesty is most important, remember. Did you smoke last night?" I asked again.

"Yeah," Lamar said as he exhaled loudly.

"And you knew you couldn't smoke marijuana while in this program, and you did it anyway," I stated.

"Uh-huh," Lamar responded.

"So you understand that you can't stay here anymore, and you have nowhere to live," I clarified.

Lamar nodded yes.

"Do you think you are unable to stop smoking?" I asked him.

Lamar shrugged.

I explained that his only other option that I was aware of—if he had no friends or family to stay with—was a rehabilitation facility through the Salvation Army down south. Lamar seemed unsure. "I understand that it's just marijuana, but you have now jeopardized your housing four times to keep smoking," I stated. "And since you continue to smoke knowing that it will result in homelessness, I think that indicates a problem," I continued.

Lamar hesitated for a while and eventually agreed to go to the treatment facility, knowing that he had no other housing options.

His caseworker and I spent the remainder of the morning securing his bed and arranging transportation to the facility. When he was finally dropped off at the Salvation Army around 8:00 p.m., Lamar called me. "I'm not going in. This program is six months! I'm not doing it. We can't even have our phones here. I would rather be in the streets!" he yelled.

After explaining that nobody was going to be able to drive back to Fort Wayne to pick him up and that he already exhausted every shelter option in the area and would be living outside if he didn't check himself into the facility, I told Lamar that I wasn't going to argue anymore and that I hoped he made the right decision before hanging up and praying that he went inside.

A few minutes later, Lamar texted me, "I'm not going in. I can't. It's just too long." Out of options and at my wits' end, I did not reply but kept hoping and praying that he would go inside. An hour later,

Lamar texted, "I went inside."

The following morning, one of the facility managers called me and said Lamar had a meltdown when he arrived the previous night but that they had him talk to their counselor, and he agreed to work the program. "I'm not optimistic that he will choose to work the program, but we'll give him a try," the manager said. I thanked him profusely.

Just one week later, Lamar texted me that he had left the facility. I asked if he went to the big homeless shelter down the road, to which he responded that he did. "I got a job at McDonald's and want to finish my classes online," he texted me.

While Lamar checks in every now and again, he remains vague about where he is or how things are going. I received an email notification from an "@drugfreewestwide" email address that someone was trying to access Lamar's résumé that I had helped him create, which I hope to be a sign that he is once again tied in with a program for young adults that may be able to help him become stable.

# CONCLUSION

As is evident throughout the boys' stories, numerous factors increase the likelihood that youth will become involved in the juvenile justice system, repeatedly cycle into and out of the system, and eventually find themselves waived to the adult justice system. Many of these factors are related to their upbringing, past abuse, neglect, and other traumas, as well as the fact that many of them know no other way of life.

As youth enter the justice system, they often begin to view themselves as "bad" or "delinquent," demonstrating the mirroring effect: "I am what I think that you think I am." As Goffman (1957) explains, we often wear different masks in order to fit into society's expectations. When youth have been told over and over again that they are useless or that they will be in the system forever, they quickly begin to believe these statements. Therefore, they begin to act in accordance with how they believe other people expect them to act.

Many additional barriers make it impossible for a majority of these young people to ever officially exit and remain uninvolved in the justice system. For example, as we saw in Elias's case, it is incredibly difficult to obtain a state ID without a matching birth certificate and social security card, two of which are needed in order to gain legal employment. A lack of reliable transportation, particularly within communities where buses do not run, makes it even more difficult for individuals to obtain and maintain gainful employment, as we saw in Jason's case.

General strain theory (Agnew, 1993) explains that when individuals fail to achieve important societal goals and are rejected by prosocial groups, they often experience decreased self-esteem, which then increases their risk of dropping out of school, behaving violently, and demonstrating delinquent and/or illegal behaviors. We see this is nearly each boy's story, as they fail to obtain jobs, driver's licenses, social status, and so on, due to the many barriers they face.

Sykes and Matza (1957) provide another explanation behind the difficulties experienced by many formerly incarcerated people in their situational theory of delinquency. They note that antisocial behavior is present only in contexts when the criminal identity is present. Sykes and Matza suggest that individuals transition between prosocial and antisocial behaviors, depending upon one's peers and environment. Sykes and Matza propose that antisocial behavior occurs only when the criminal identity is present. Therefore, individuals are more likely to exhibit delinquent behaviors when they are in the presence of others who exhibit such behaviors. As we can see through this book, several of the young people described are interconnected with one another, even if they do not reside in the same county and were not locked up together within the same facility.

Lifestyles and habits are simply hard to break, particularly as we grow older. Many young people who were not taught positive coping or life skills early on find it increasingly difficult to break old patterns and adopt new ways of life as they grow older. For some, the financial burdens and sense of responsibility they feel to care for themselves, their families, and others result in them determining that the risk of incarceration is simply worth the money that they can make selling drugs. "Why would I struggle to find a job when I wouldn't make nearly as much money as I'm making now?" several young people have asked me when we talk about career options. For many, they do not even know what a stable household, gainful employment, or a loving family look like. Therefore, how can we simply expect them to reach these goals at our urging?

While society tends to write off justice-system-involved youth as "bad" or "career criminals," it is critical that we recognize the traumatic backgrounds, negative influences, and overall adverse environments experienced by a majority of incarcerated and formerly incarcerated people. These young people who are often somewhat purposefully ignored and/or criticized by society are the same vulnerable youth who have been failed by many systems throughout the entirety of their lives. They are being labeled as and subsequently internalizing the labels of "juvenile delinquents" and/or "felons," and the eventual reversal and redefining of norms are often present in the youths' stories as well.

As Boduszek and Hyland (2011) describe, such labels and discrimination frequently influence youth to seek acceptance and harden themselves to the feelings of marginalization from those who conform to mainstream society. Finally, the formation of criminal norms and concerns regarding their reputation often also appear to play a role in the formation of a criminal identity among justice-involved youth. We see this desire to protect themselves and their reputations repeatedly throughout the stories of youth included in this study, as they essentially don a mask and present themselves differently when they feel the need to defend their reputation as "hard" and uncaring about what the rest of society thinks of them.

However, it is also important to note that prosocial identities were demonstrated at some point by all juveniles included in this study. According to Boduszek and Hyland (2011), situation-specific schemas can result in the development of multiple social identities, including both prosocial and criminal identities. It is apparent throughout the entirety of the study that context—including who is present, the physical environment, and any immediately former occurrences—is critical in shaping the thoughts, speech, and behaviors of youth. Many of the juveniles included in the study were able to "take off their mask" when they were speaking alone with me, while they appeared to feel the need to portray themselves as "hard" when surrounded by peers who also exhibited criminal identities.

It is also important to note that participants in the study seemed to be more apt to demonstrate prosocial behaviors even when they were around other peers, so long as their peers also were exhibiting prosocial behaviors. For example, in the cases of Hector and Elias, Hector altered his behaviors and began talking about his excitement to begin attending school when he was in conversation with another boy enrolled in the same school and while visiting with Elias, as Elias was adamant about adhering to society's expectations of him upon release from the county jail.

In interactions such as these, it appears that REACH participants demonstrate prosocial and criminal identities throughout the study, depending upon the current environment and who is present in each context. However, as Boduszek and Hyland (2011) explain in their model of the criminal social identity, the existence of situation-specific schemas and multiple social identities should indicate the expectation that REACH participants naturally will demonstrate both progressions and regressions in terms of behaviors throughout their involvement in the program. Rather than taking antisocial behavior as a sign that mentoring does not work among the population, it is critical that such behaviors instead be recognized as normal and utilized to inform the construction of effective mentoring programs and activities conducted within reentry efforts.

Nevertheless, it is also important to recognize the fact that even when youth are provided with mentoring, support, guidance, and resources, it is still to be expected that they will regress and often continue struggling with issues that initially led to their incarceration. The fluidity and frequent shift between prosocial behavior and antisocial behavior should not be taken as a sign of failure or as resources being wasted on youth who cannot be helped. Rather, the progress made should be interpreted as a signifier of the malleability of youth, even after becoming involved in the juvenile justice system. Positive influences and support can still have a positive impact, perhaps even especially among incarcerated and formerly incarcerated teens who crave the love, attention, and support that many of them have been denied for a majority of their lives. As we often say in the social work field, "We must measure our success in moments."

# CALL TO ACTION

Thank you for taking the time to read the stories of just several of the millions of Americans whose lives have been impacted by the justice system. If you want to join our team of people who seek to provide support, encouragement, and resources to help those justice-involved individuals like the boys described throughout this book, please send me an email at samantha.burgett@communitychangecenter.org or engage through our website at www.communitychangecenter.org or Facebook at https://www.facebook.com/CommunityChangeCenterWeAreOne. Together, we can change the narrative and break the cycle of crime, violence, and incarceration plaguing our communities. Thank you for caring about those who are often forgotten.

# REFERENCES

Agnew, R. (1993). Why do they do it? An examination of the intervening mechanisms between "social control" variables and delinquency. *Journal of Research in Crime and Delinquency*, 30, 245–266.

Boduszek, D., & Hyland, P. (2011). The theoretical model of criminal social identity: Psycho-social perspective. *International Journal of Criminology and Sociological Theory*, 4(1), 604–615. http://ijcst.journals.yorku.ca/index.php/ijcst/article/view/32125.

Goffman, I. (1956). The presentation of self in everyday life. Doubleday.

Sawyer, W. (2019). Youth confinement: The whole pie 2019. Prison Policy Initiative. https://www.prisonpolicy.org/reports/youth2019.html.

Sykes, G. M., & Matza, D. (1957). Techniques of neutralization: A theory of delinquency. *American Sociological Review*, 22, 664–670.

# ABOUT THE AUTHOR

In 2017, Samantha Burgett was running a teen program in Northwest Indiana, when she noticed several of her youth demonstrating new negative behaviors after having been incarcerated in the local juvenile detention center for a short period of time. Feeling called to address the issues she was observing, Sam, along with one of her professors and a close friend, launched a mentoring program in the detention center. After running the program in the facility for a few short months, Sam began working at the agency as a detention officer and quickly noticed many gaps in the American justice system. After studying reentry programs around the world, Sam launched an intensive reentry program within the facility, working with the older youth and young adults while they were detained and, for those who were interested, as they returned back to the community. Shortly after, the opportunity arose to launch a similar group in the local prison, providing reentry programming to incarcerated adults in the community. In order to funnel more resources into the programs and to be able to offer more services to program participants, Sam founded a nonprofit, the Community Change Center, in 2019. Today, the Center operates reentry programming in local correctional facilities and provides community-based reintegration services to individuals as they are released from incarceration, including transitional living, adult education, mentoring, case management, expungement fairs, and a Unity Cafe.

www.ingramcontent.com/pod-product-compliance
Lightning Source LLC
Chambersburg PA
CBHW031419120626
46545CB00006B/2178